THE INDIANS ALWAYS WIN
A Primer on Indian Law

LANTZ McCLAIN

Published in the USA

INDIE
PUB
PRESS

Indie Pub Press

ISBN -13: 978-1-951772-57-4

TABLE OF CONTENTS

"Take the time to walk a mile in his moccasins."

1 – THE INDIANS ARE DIFFERENT

F. Scott Fitzgerald is supposed to have said, "The rich are different from you and me." To which Ernest Hemingway is supposed to have replied, "Right, they've got more money." The Indians are different from you and me, too. They've got more legal privileges. Having more money and more privileges are closely related.

Black's Law Dictionary rather ponderously defines a "privilege" as, "A particular and peculiar advantage enjoyed by a person, company, or class, beyond the common advantages of other citizens." What do you expect from a legal dictionary? More straightforward, we might say a "legal privilege" simply a legal right (or power) other people don't have.

A legal privilege closely relates to what economists call "rent-seeking," manipulating the political system to redistribute wealth without creating any value in return. By contrast, "profit-seeking" (as the term used by economists) creates wealth by adding value. Profit-seeking is mutually beneficial, but rent-seeking is profiteering at the public expense. Profit-seeking leads to efficiency, innovation, and economic growth, but rent-seeking has the opposite effects.

For a classic example of how legal privileges and rent-seeking go together, say a river ran through a nobleman's domain (which many did in the long ago). Say the nobleman stretched a chain across the channel (which he had the legal right to do in those days). Now the merchant vessels plying the river had to pay a toll to pass his chain. The nobleman was profit-seeking all right, but that was rent-seeking. He was using a legal privilege to redistribute some wealth from the merchants' pockets into his own coffers. He wasn't adding any value, only driving up the cost of doing business. By contrast, a downriver miller might build a mill with a wheel turned by the current. He was profit-seeking, too, but not rent-seeking. His mill added something of value.

"Ye'll take the high road and I'll take the low road." Throughout history, whoever could cram on board has traveled these lower roads (to legal privileges and rent-seeking) as the fast track to the high road (where they can ride in the first-class carriages). Indian law long ago went down this same path.

How did that happen? It's complicated. It's the law of unforeseen consequences in action. It's the law of misguided good intentions in action. Above all, it's Hobbes old primary law of political action. "So that in the first place, I put for a general inclination of all mankind, a perpetual and restless desire of Power after power." In other words, it's the law of self-interest in action.

Until today, a vast gathering of interests feed on (and so support) these legal privileges. It's the familiar iron triangle – the Indians (and those feeding on the Indians), the federal bureaucracy (a growth feeding on the Indians), and Congress (who fund the meal, dining themselves on the generous campaign contributions fed back to them by the other diners). Reinforcing this structure from the outside, the legal profession (the most powerful interest group in America) provide the (legal) buttresses. Indian law serves as a huge power source for judges and a highly lucrative revenue stream for lawyers.

What are the Indians present legal privileges? That's complicated, too, which part of the problem. It's so complicated no one knows quite what the Indian laws are. But to give a generalized and partial list of their privileges no one else has, most obviously perhaps, Indian casinos where no one else has the right to have a casino. Their casinos and other businesses are tax exempt, but they can tax non-Indians on their reservations (that income also tax exempt to them). They possess vast lands, theirs in perpetuity and non-taxable. They possess the income from the natural resources on those lands (also tax free). Individual Indians enjoy tax emptions as well. Often a state can't prosecute them for crimes. They can hunt and fish with no license, no regulation, and no limit. The tribes have sovereign immunity (can't be sued over their contracts or debts). Indians have free health care, housing, and education. Perhaps this list long enough to make a start, and we might add it's a growing list, with new rights (and privileges) found and added all the time.

Indians are different from you and me. They've got more legal privileges. It's complicated. My purpose in these articles is to unravel the story. How did Indian law take the path to privilege? Where did the path lead? Might we find a better path?

2 – THE PATH OF INDIAN LAW

In America, we pride ourselves on following the path of "the rule of law." But what, exactly, is "the law" or "the rule of law?" While since we're on the subject, how does Indian law follow that same path (or does it)?

The English philosopher John Austin (lived 1790 to 1859) gave a famous definition of the law. "Every law ... is a command. ... The evil which will probably be incurred in case a command be disobeyed ... is frequently called a sanction." That backs into it with sufficient lawyerly caution. More simply put, a law is a command backed with the threat of a punishment. "Don't do the crime, if you can't do the time." But later legal commentators added to his definition, noting not all laws have a sanction (a punishment). Rather, a lot of laws only define legal rights or set forth legal procedures. The law against murder is backed by a punishment, but the law for a jury trial only provides a procedure to determine whether the accused guilty or not. The law of intestate succession provides who inherits in the absence of a will (defines their legal rights), and other probate law set forth the procedure to determine who the rightful heirs.

If "the law" either a command (backed by a punishment), defines legal rights, or sets forth legal procedures, what's "the rule of law?" Still another English legal philosopher, A.V. Dicey (lived 1835 to 1922), receives the credit for popularizing the phrase "the rule of law." Again like a good lawyer, he backs into it cautiously enough, beginning this way, "We mean, ... that no man is punished or … made to suffer in body or goods except for a distinct breach of law established in the ordinary legal manner before the ordinary Courts of the land."

Sorting through this caution, "the rule of law" begins with two requirements. First, if "no man is punished … except for a distinct breach of the law," the law must be distinctly stated, that is, with enough clarity a breach can be clearly "established" (clearly seen). Second, if "no man is to be punished except for a distinct breach of the law established in the ordinary legal manner," the "ordinary legal manner" of proceeding against him must also be clearly "established," that is, the legal procedures must also be clearly set out and fair (so we clearly follow the procedures to reach reliably fair verdicts).

But there's a third crucial requirement. Dicey goes on, "We mean … when we speak of the 'rule of law' … not only that … no man is above the law, but … every man, whatever be his rank or condition, is subject to the ordinary law of the realm … ." In other words, everyone has the same standing before and treated the same by the law (that is, "equal protection of the laws").

In sum, to follow the path of "the rule of law" we have to follow three guideposts, 1) distinctly (clearly) stated laws, 2) established (clear and fair) procedures, and 3) everyone treated the same (equal protection). Otherwise, we're going to wander off the path.

Why is following this path so important? In the first place, as Dicey goes on to say, "[T]he rule of law is contrasted with every system of government based on the exercise by persons in authority of wide, arbitrary, or discretionary powers." And that's obvious, isn't it? If your "system of government" doesn't follow the rule of law, the "persons in authority" have an open path to "wide, arbitrary, or discretionary powers." The law not being clear, the procedures not being clear and fair, everyone not treated the same, the law will simply follow whatever path those authorities prefer when sitting in judgment (and you can be sure their verdicts will prefer them over you).

In the second place, without the rule of law you can't rely on the laws to live your life and do your business. If the law not clearly stated, you can't know how to abide by it. If the procedures not clearly set out and fair, you can't know they'll lead to reliably fair verdicts. If everyone not treated equal, you can't know how they'll treat you. So you find no safety there. Rather than bringing some order out of chaos, you're left adrift on a sea of uncertainty, where rational decision-making has to look for some other reasons outside the law (which usually amounts to courting the wide, arbitrary, and discretionary power of the authorities).

It should be obvious, then, that the rule of law stands as a foundational (and fundamental) principle in our American democracy. "All men are created equal ... with certain unalienable rights." How without the rule of law?

And so, the U.S. Constitution enshrines the rule of law. The 5th and 14th Amendments guarantee, "No person shall be ... deprived of life, liberty, or property, without due process of law." This "due process clause" embodies the first two requirements of the rule of law – clearly stated laws and clearly established and fair procedures. Further, nor shall the government "deny to any person within its jurisdiction the equal protection of the laws." This "equal protection clause" embodies the third requirement – equal standing before and equal treatment by the law.

To come back to the other question asked, How does Indian law follow that same path (or does it)? And, no, it doesn't. The rule of law stands like a three-legged stool, but Indian law standing at most on one leg. It's missing the first leg. It's not clearly stated. Often you can only find the Indian law after years of costly litigation, and what seemed a part of the leg can suddenly crumble beneath you. But at least when you're in the federal courts, it has the second leg. The federal courts have clear and fair procedures. But above all, it's permanently missing the third leg. Indian law denies the "equal protection of the laws," giving Indians special legal privileges no one else has.

Not to mince words, Indian law doesn't follow the path of the rule of law, but has gone down the path to privilege. By so doing, it has come to violate both the due process and equal protection guaranteed by the U.S. Constitution. Let's see how in the following articles.

3 – THE GREAT FATHER'S HOUSE

So far, the Indian tribes haven't escaped entirely from the Great Father's house, nor do they want to entirely. "In my father's house are many mansions." They've come to occupy some of the prime locations and mean to occupy some more. But the Great Father's infrastructure and economy give those prime locations their value, and leaving the house would leave behind his deep pockets (in which they've been known to dip their fingers). Instead, they're willing to compromise. For their share of the Great Father's inheritance, they're willing to stay just far enough inside the family business to share the profits, while edging just far enough outside to avoid the investments and operating costs. As has been remarked, "Indians always were politically savvy."

But as long as they stay inside the Great Father's house, the U.S. Constitution remains the basic rule for the occupants. We always hear the Constitution grants the government only enumerated powers. Under the shade of which enumerations has the vast undergrowth of the present Indian laws grown up? Usually, the first mentioned is "the treaty making power," which says, "He [the president] shall have Power, by and with the Advice and Consent of the Senate, to make Treaties." Next mentioned is the "Indian commerce clause," which says, The Congress shall have Power ... To regulate Commerce ... with the Indian Tribes." Also mentioned are the congressional powers to govern the territories and to tax and spend "for the ... general Welfare of the United States."

Whether the Indian tribes like it or not, these enumerations leave the Great Father with a whole lot of parental authority over them. As the Supreme Court said in a fairly recent case (U.S. v Lara from 2001), "the Constitution grants Congress broad general powers to legislate in respect to Indian tribes, powers that we have consistently described as 'plenary and exclusive.'" Plenary means "full" power. Exclusive means to the exclusion of the states, who've got absolutely no power over Indian law (unless the feds give it to them). In other words, the Great Father still runs his house, even the wings occupied by the tribes.

That's clear enough in the legal theory, but the legal practice so complex as only a lawyer could love. Just enumerating all the Indian laws serves as a quick tip off. The leading text, *Cohen's Handbook of Federal Indian Law* says, "Congress ... has enacted over four thousand treaties and statutes dealing with Native Americans. [Bureaucratic] [r]egulations and guidelines implementing these laws are even more numerous. The tribes' own laws, and some state statutes dealing with Indians, add to the complexity. There are thousands of reported judicial decisions in Indian law." That's a lot of laws. No wonder *Cohen's Handbook* now runs to about 1,500 pages and looks about ready to break into two volumes with the next edition.

More specifically, there are only about 400 Indian treaties. But that's only because Congress quit making treaties in 1871. Remember, the treaty making power is confined to the president and the Senate. Being cut out of the process (and so out of the power) offended the House of Representatives. They made their displeasure effectively felt, and formal treaty making ended. But treaty making didn't stop. Instead, Congress (in effect) began making treaties by passing statutes, and they've passed dozens. In addition, the presidents have often made treaties by simply signing executive orders (of which there are hundreds). Adding to that, the federal bureaucracy has enacted thousands of regulations to carry out the statutes and orders. Even though, as said, the states lack all power over Indian law, the feds have sometimes granted them some authority, and so, they've passed hundreds of laws, too. Adding still another layer, the tribes have come to make their own tribal laws (in the thousands). To top it all off, the courts (and of course, most prominently the Supreme Court) have handed down thousands of decisions, telling everybody else what their laws meant (or what the justices think they should have meant).

And it's a legal Tower of Babble, but what would you expect? With so many laws made by so many hands over so much time, who should expect a coherent architectural design with well laid bricks? One era built on one blueprint and the next redrew the plans. From about 1887 to 1928, the fashion in design called for allotment and assimilation (allotting the tribal lands to individual Indians and assimilating them like bricks into the national structure). From the 1960s to the present, the fashion altered to self-determination (creating tribal governments to design their own buildings). While all the time, these many hands have drawn their plans and laid their bricks with their own interests in mind.

No wonder confusion reigns, and no doubt confusion reigns. If you want a definite answer about a question of Indian law (something on which quite a bit of money and power often hangs), get ready for years of costly litigation. One complicated and long-drawn out case leads to another complicated and long-drawn out case. Answers previously taken for granted (sometimes for over a century) suddenly turn into wrong answers. Only a lawyer could love this.

But let's not forget we're still in the Great Father's house. The U.S. Constitution still sets forth the basic rules. Whether the Indian tribes like it or not (and they don't), the

U.S. government still has "plenary" (full) power over them and Indian law. But what would they have? Far from a domestic tyrant, the Great Father runs his house by fair rules. The Constitution not only grants him power, but restrains his power. Although many of the tenants a disorderly lot, constantly complaining about their accommodations, nobody else runs a more prosperous house with more rights for the tenants.

But let's not forget another and basic rule in the Great Father's house. "All men are created equal." If we're equal in the house, we should all live by the same rules. But we don't. However confused and complicated the Indian law, it clearly violates this most basic rule. As the following articles will show, the Indians have all sorts of legal privileges the other occupants don't have. If someone should be complaining about the Great Father, it's not them.

4 – AS LONG AS THE GRASS SHALL GROW

Throughout the cases and commentary on Indian law, you'll never see a reference to Indian "privileges." Rather, you'll always see their privileges called their "rights." It certainly sounds better to say your rights rather than your privileges. Everyone thinks you're entitled to your rights, but not so many that you're entitled to special privileges. "I demand my rights!" Who doesn't? What's a more popular demand? But by now we should know there's also nothing more popular than claiming some legal privilege disguised as some legal right. The Indians are at the head of one of these lines.

But Indian rights didn't start out as legal privileges, although they had an unusual start. American law starts with the U.S. Constitution, which generated all the federal and state laws. But Indian law starts with the Indian treaties. The Indian tribes want to claim their treaties make them into virtually independent nations. But for all the confusion about the Indian law, that's not the law, never was the law, and never can be the law (whatever the confusion of some of the language). If it's to remain "one nation, indivisible," the Indian law can't divide them out from under the Constitution (and it doesn't).

The confusion comes from loosely throwing around the notion of "a treaty." In the first place, a lot of the so-called Indian treaties aren't even treaties. Formal treaty making with the tribes ended in 1871, but informal treaty making proceeded apace (through laws passed by Congress and executive orders issued by the president). And congressional laws and executive orders remain subject to change.

In the second place, even regarding the Indian treaties as falling under the international law of treaties, the result would be the same. Under the Vienna Convention of Treaties, "A treaty … is not subject to denunciation or withdrawal unless: *(a)* It is established that the parties intended to admit the possibility of denunciation or withdrawal; or (b) A right of denunciation or withdrawal may be implied by the nature of the treaty." In addition, there's a third reason, "A fundamental change of circumstances which has occurred with regard to those existing at the time of the conclusion of a treaty, and which was not foreseen by the parties."

American law has always regarded the Indian treaties as both, (a) intended to admit the possibility of change, and (b) having a right to change implied by their nature. In addition, fundamental changes of circumstances have often occurred not foreseen at the time. So the treaties were always regarded as subject to change.

For an example we will encounter again, in the 1830s, the U.S. signed treaties with the Five Tribes (the Cherokee, Chickasaw, Choctaw, Creek, and Seminole) granting them extensive reservations in what later the State of Oklahoma. Each tribe governed their own reservation. However, after the Civil War, thousands of settlers flooded into these reservations, ranching, and farming, and towns sprang up all along the railroad lines across the reservations. By 1900, the over 300,000 settlers outnumbered the members of Five Tribes by 3 to 1. So the circumstances having changed, Congress changed the treaties. They did away with the tribal governments and admitted Oklahoma as a state (the forty-sixth, in 1907).

Thus, as the Supreme Court would state the law in the Lone Wolf Case (back in 1903), "Plenary authority over the tribal relations of the Indians has been exercised by

Congress from the beginning." "Plenary" means as full as it can be. More specifically, the Court went on, "The power exists to abrogate the provisions of an Indian treaty, ... When, therefore, treaties were entered into between the United States and a tribe of Indians, it was never doubted that the power to abrogate existed in Congress, and that, in a contingency, such power might be availed of from considerations of governmental policy, particularly if consistent with perfect good faith towards the Indians."

In other words, an Indian treaty might contain some such words as, "for as long as the grass shall grow and the waters flow." And so, the common view prevails and the Indian tribes want to argue that the treaties were forever. All that remains is for the U.S. to live up to its word (as the Indians interpret it and forever). But anyone familiar with the actual law knows that's not correct and never was correct. Having given its word, the U.S. government (or anybody else) shouldn't lightly go back on it. But as we just heard the Court say, when circumstances arise that justify a change (or even abrogation) of a treaty, Congress can change it just like they can change any other law. Whatever confusion may exist in the common mind or whatever the tribes want to argue, that's always been the law.

But the tribes don't like this law. Their advocates are waging a constant campaign urging a repeal. Their stuff fills the bar journals and academic press, where they never met a further Indian right (which they never call a privilege) not to love. They're not too specific about what they want instead. But apparently, they long to erect the tribes into some sort of semi-independent mini-nations. But be careful what you wish for. American law starts with the U.S. Constitution, which not only grants the government power, but restrains the government. If the tribes escape from the federal government's power, what any longer restrains their tribal governments?

Those who don't think this a problem forget their history. For an example in the law books, we mentioned the Five Tribes (or Five Civilized Tribes), who long governed themselves on their reservations in what now Oklahoma. With respect to that period, in U.S. v Mitchell (1983), the Supreme Court said, "[T]he reports of the Dawes Commission show conclusively that the governments of the Five Civilized Tribes were notoriously and incurably corrupt, that every branch of the service was infested with favoritism, graft and crookedness, and that, by such methods, the tribal officers acquired large fortunes, while the other members entitled to share in the tribal income received little benefit therefrom." The Dawes Commission (named after its first chairman, Henry F. Dawes) refers to an outfit set up by Congress back in 1893 to look into the condition of the Five Tribes (among other things).

If you're a non-Indian, you better think again before the tribes escape from the Constitution. If they escape, what protects you from their tribal governments (when you cross over into Indian country)? The Indians themselves better think again, too. What's going to protect them from their tribal governments? If they escape the Constitution, are they escaping to someplace with more and better protected rights? Where would that be?

5 – THE INDIANS ALWAYS WIN

When lawyers talk about the "canons of construction," they're talking about the rules to interpret the law. For example, one standard rule says the courts should interpret the laws in keeping with the legislative intent. Otherwise, the judges could frustrate the purpose for which the legislature passed the law. The fact such intent sometimes hard to determine or the fact the judges sometimes willfully ignore it (to substitute their judicial purpose for the legislative purpose) are beside the point. The rule remains, makes good sense, and a good rule.

But when it comes to Indian law, there's a whole set of special rules, radically different from the rules applied to others. Called "Cohen's canons of construction," these are named for Felix S. Cohen (lived 1907 to 1953). Called "the Blackstone of American Indian law" (comparing him to Sir William Blackstone, whose *Commentaries on the Laws of England*, published in four volumes back in 1765 to 1770, had an immense influence on Anglo-American law), Cohen had more influence on the development of Indian law than anyone else. Coming to Washington from legal academia as a New Deal "brain-truster," he served in the Office of the Solicitor General in the Department of the Interior from 1933 to 1946. From this vantage point, he was one of the prime architects of the "Indian New Deal" (about which more in a later article).

As for the weight of his hand on the scales of justice, in 1950s, Cohen wrote, "the Indian plays much the same role in our American society that the Jews played in Germany.

Like the miner's canary, the Indian marks the shift from fresh air to poison gas in our political atmosphere." Being himself Jewish, this pretty much tells you which side he threw his weight on. *Cohen's Handbook of Federal Indians Law* was first published in 1941, has been republished and updated since, and now up to over 1,500 pages, which looks about ready to break into two volumes. Talk about a ponderous tome. It's the standard text. Fair to say, it not only covers the story of Indian law, but covers the story from the view most favorable to the Indians, faithfully advocating for them throughout.

In this vein, Cohen states the rules for the interpretation of Indian law as follows, "The theory and interpretation in federal Indian law differs from that of other fields of law. … The basic Indian law canons of construction require that treaties, agreements, statutes, and executive orders be liberally construed in favor of the Indians, and that all ambiguities be resolved in their favor. In addition, treaties and agreements are to be construed as the Indians would have understood them, and tribal property rights and sovereignty are preserved unless Congress's intent to the contrary is clear and unambiguous." There you have "Cohen's Canons."

If that doesn't go far enough, there's another unspoken canon. As one famous lawyer who won a series of cases for his Indian clients gleefully remarked, "The Indians always win." That unspoken rule says it all.

The case of Choctaw Nation v Oklahoma (decided by the Supreme Court in 1970) provides a good example of how Cohen's Canons work in practice. At stake was the ownership to the riverbed of the Arkansas River in Oklahoma, which to say, the valuable minerals (such as oil and gas) and the dry land created by navigation projects that had narrowed and deepened the channel. In 1966, the Cherokee Nation filed a lawsuit claiming this land belonged to them rather than the State of Oklahoma. The

Choctaw and Chickasaw Nations soon joined in.
Way back in the 1830s, the U.S. had signed treaties with these tribes, granting them vast stretches of land in what then only a territory, not yet a state. However, later in 1898, Congress provided for the allotment of the lands among the tribal members, leaving only small parcels in the name of the tribes. Then in 1907, Oklahoma was admitted as the forty-sixth state. As for the Arkansas River, the navigable channel ran through the lands previously granted to the tribes. When the riverbed eventually acquired some value (as seen by 1966), someone (perhaps a clever lawyer looking to scare up a fee) came up with a bright idea. Why not claim (what seemed a farfetched claim at the time) that this land belonged to the tribes?

Under the ordinary rules of construction, the riverbed looked to belong to the State of Oklahoma, and the law looked pretty clear. Way back in 1796 Congress passed a law that, "All navigable rivers, within the territory occupied by the public lands, shall remain and be deemed public highways." As a result, when the U.S. grants land to a state, a tribe, or whoever, it doesn't matter what it says in the grant, no one can block the navigable parts of a river. Why? Because otherwise they could just stretch a chain across the river and start charging a toll, interfering with the free flow of interstate commerce. In addition, the U.S. also retains the title to the riverbed. As said in the case, "conveyances by the United States of land located on a navigable river carry no interest in the river bed under federal law."

As the next step in the ordinary rules of construction, when Congress admits a new state, the state succeeds to the U.S. title to the riverbed (although of course, it still can't block navigation on the river). As the Court stated this rule in a 1981 case (Montana v US), "[C]onveyance by the United States of land riparian to [on the banks of] a navigable river carries no interest in the riverbed. ... the Federal Government holds such lands in trust for future

States, to be granted to such States when they enter the Union and assume sovereignty on an 'equal footing' with the established States. ... The State's power over the beds of navigable waters remains subject to only one limitation: the paramount power of the United States to ensure that such waters remain free to interstate and foreign commerce."

It must follow, then, that under the settled rules of construction, Oklahoma succeeded to the U.S. title to riverbed on admission as a state. But wait for it. The Supreme Court will apply Cohen's Canons. They say, "this Court has often held that treaties with the Indians must be interpreted as they would have understood them, ... and any doubtful expressions in them should be resolved in the Indians' favor." Now since the riverbed had no value at the time, even interpreting the treaties as "they would have understood them" (at the time), there appears no reason the Indians would have given any thought to it. Even resolving the "doubtful expressions" in their favor, where are the doubtful expressions?

But no matter. The Indians always win, and they won this case, too. Rather than all the people in Oklahoma benefiting from the Arkansas riverbed, now just the ones in these Indian tribes have all the benefit.

If you're going to start out down the path to legal privilege, you couldn't pick a better place to start than with the rules that guide the interpretation of the law. If those rules always guide the interpretation toward your favor, you've made a good start at going down the path to laws privileged in your favor. That's where the Indian law starts. No wonder the Indians always win.

6 – Breaking Back in the Reservation

Used to be the Indians would break out of the reservation, but now they want to break back in. Most recently (in 2020), the Creek Tribe in Oklahoma pulled off this feat. No story better illustrates what's wrong with Indian law.

This particular story starts with a couple Indians committing some rather heinous crimes off the reservation. At least, everyone thought they were off the reservation, since everyone thought the reservation long gone (for over a century). It ends with them breaking back in the reservation (and taking a lot of other Indians with them). That happened in 2020, when the Supreme Court (in the McGirt Case, a five to four decision) ruled that the reservation had been there all along. The Indians broke back in by finding out they had never left. Everyone had just been confused about the law all these years (apparently including the four dissenting justices, who were still confused). With this ruling, the reservation reappeared and the convictions disappeared.

The case started out back in 1997 (already twenty years gone by), when one Jimcy McGirt, a Seminole, was charged in Oklahoma state court with molesting, sodomizing, and raping a four-year old girl. The jury returned a verdict of guilty with sentences totaling 1,000 years. In 1999, in another case that would become connected during the appeal process, another Indian, this time a Creek, one Patrick Dwayne Murphy, slit another guy's throat, cut off his genitals, and left him in a ditch to bleed to death. Charged with murder in the Oklahoma state courts, the jury returned the death penalty.

The facts apparently not leaving their defense lawyers much to work with, they (naturally) started looking for some technical out. Indian law being so confused, that's always a good place to start looking for such technicalities. Pouring over the fine print, they came up with what seemed a farfetched argument.

Not maybe widely known (although these cases would eventually make it more widely known), an Indian who commits a crime in "Indian country" (which includes a reservation) often has a special status. The criminal laws of the state don't apply to him, only the federal laws. The state can't charge him with the crime, only the feds. That rule varies among the states depending on some legal circumstances too complicated to go into at present, but that's the rule in Oklahoma.

Already having said that the State of Oklahoma (not the feds) prosecuted Murphy and McGirt, we need add only one more ingredient. Both men committed their crimes on lands formerly part of the Creek Indian Reservation. Formerly, because everyone thought that reservation had gone out of existence over a century past. For all that time, Oklahoma had been prosecuting Indians (and everyone else) for crimes committed there. But since Indian law so confused, the lawyers came up with an argument to exploit the confusion. They argued everyone had been wrong all these years and the reservation still existed. All those thousands of prosecutions had violated the Indians' rights (their legal privileges to be prosecuted only in federal court). While that seemed a farfetched argument, when it came to Indian law, they well knew such arguments had often succeeded. Then why not see if they could persuade the federal courts to swallow the argument and rule the Creek Reservation never went out of existence? From their point of view, there was no harm in trying.

You see where this was headed. If Murphy and McGirt

had committed their crimes on the reservation, Oklahoma had violated their Indian rights (their privilege against prosecution in the state's courts). If their defense lawyer's argument won, their legal privileges would vacate the legality of their convictions.

At which point the Creek Tribe and some other tribes in Oklahoma began to get excited about this argument themselves. If Murphy and McGirt could break back in the reservation, they wanted to go right along with them. Why? Because of all the (other) special legal privileges Indians have on the reservation they don't have off. Joining in by filing *amicus curie* (friend of the court) briefs, several of the tribes urged the federal courts to go along with the argument.

And sure enough, Indian law proved hopelessly confused once again. In the 2020 McGirt Case, the Supreme Court reversed what seemed settled law for over a century. Everyone had been wrong all that time. McGirt, Murphy, and the tribes all broke back in the reservation, since it turned out they had never left. The convictions of McGirt and Murphy were dismissed, since their legal privilege to be prosecuted in the federal rather than the state courts had been violated. As for the tribes, all their special legal privileges that come from being on the reservation were restored.

Almost as a footnote, McGirt and Murphy haven't yet gone free. The charges were refilled in federal court. But at least they got another bite at the apple. Who knows, after so many years, maybe some evidence will have gone missing or some witnesses died. Maybe there are some other technical arguments their defense lawyers can make. Maybe the juries will be more sympathetic this time. As for Murphy, there's no federal death penalty for Indian crimes in federal court, so at least he's doesn't have to face that.

Why does this story show what's wrong with Indian law? Just on the surface it doesn't look too savory. Two guys who committed bad crimes got their convictions reversed, although the authorities did nothing they could have known was wrong and McGirt and Murphy were treated no different than anyone else. But when we look beneath the surface, there's a lot more wrong. Let start looking in the next article.

7 – IMAGINING A RESERVATION

In the last article we saw the Supreme Court rule (in the McGirt Case in 2020) that the Creek Reservation (and by implication, a number of other Indian reservations in Oklahoma) never went out of existence (although everybody thought so for over a century). But not only did everyone think they went out of existence, they did go out of existence in the real world. Re-imagining them required quite a feat of legal imagination, while the overall effect of this legal make-believe in the real world isn't yet worked out.

If you drive through Nebraska or South Dakota, you may pass a Sioux reservation. Very few people other than the Sioux live there. But driving through Oklahoma, you won't see any such reservation (whether one legally exists or not). The last census (2010) showed a population of about 4,000,000 with about 400,000 Indians (10%). That's the second highest total and second highest percentage of any state. Some 38 federally recognized tribes call Oklahoma home. But before the recent Supreme Court decision reviving the reservations, only about 5% of the land still qualified as "Indian country," which mainly consisted of surviving Indian allotments scattered around like isolated squares on a checkerboard. The Indians themselves live not just on these allotments, but scattered randomly throughout the rural areas, towns, and cities. They don't just live scrambled up with the general population, they are scrambled up (through marriage and otherwise). A true full blood has become rather rare. More often than not, you can't tell an Indian by looking. To know for sure, you have to ask.

So much for the demography in the real world. And where do you see your traditional image of an Indian reservation (someplace reserved for the Indians)? Nowhere on the map. There are simply no *de facto* (as a matter of fact) reservations, however a number of *de jure* (as a matter of law) ones now exist (by judicial fiat). To say any reservation exists (as the Supreme Court did in McGirt) amounts to legal make-believe, and it's hard to live in a make-believe world. When the laws don't fit with the reality, there's probably a problem with the laws.

As for the history in the real world, back in the 1830s, the U.S. signed a treaty with the Creeks (and similar treaties with the Cherokees, Chickasaws, Choctaws, and Seminoles, together the Five Civilized Tribes or Five Tribes). These treaties set up reservations for them, covering most of the empty lands later the State of Oklahoma. These tribes ran their own tribal governments, administered their own laws, and held their lands in commonality (the tribe owned the land, not any member). But during the Civil War, some made the mistake of siding with the Confederacy (perhaps in part because they owned slaves themselves). In the treaties ending those hostilities, they were obliged to renounce slavery and their reservations were diminished to about the eastern half of the state.

"Go west, young man." In the next decades, an irresistible flood of settlers took the advice, nor did they pause at the boundaries of the Five Tribes. They moved in, homesteading, farming, and ranching. Following the railroads, towns sprang up all across the reservations. By 1900, the over 300,000 settlers outnumbered the Five Tribes by 3 to 1. But these new towns lacked governments. These new settlers lacked good title to their houses, farms, and ranches, since title to all the land still held in the name of the tribes. At the same time, complaints sounded about some of the tribal leaders profiteering at the expense of the other members, appropriating the good land for themselves. So sort of the opposite of what we saw the Supreme Court do in the McGirt Case, Congress decided to fit the law to the facts. They decided to make Oklahoma a state and make the Indians citizens the same as everyone else. In 1890, an act established a territorial government. In 1893, the Curtis Act provided for the allotment of tribal lands among individual members (conveying the title to them as individuals) and made townsites available for purchase by non-Indians. In 1906, another act essentially wound up the affairs of the tribal government. In 1907, an enabling act admitted Oklahoma as the forty-sixth state. The new state government took over, including prosecuting criminal cases against Indians (which they did for over a hundred years).

Then how in 2020, did the majority on the Supreme Court persuade themselves the Creek Reservation still existed? As usual with Indian law, it's confused and complicated. But the thin edge of the wedge was that none of these many acts "explicitly" said the reservation "disestablished."

Why not? That question has come up routinely with regard to Indian reservations all across America. Congress has seldom explicitly said a reservation disestablished. And the reason is simple. As the Supreme Court said in a leading case (Solem v Bartlett, from 1984), "the surplus land Acts themselves seldom detail whether opened lands retained reservation status or were divested of all Indian interests. When the surplus land Acts were passed, the distinction seemed unimportant. The notion that reservation status of Indian lands might not be coextensive with tribal ownership was unfamiliar at the turn of the century."

In other words, when Congress provided for allotment of Indian lands (to the individual members of the tribe), they took it for granted the act diminished or disestablished the reservation. And, "Another reason ... was the turn-of-the-century assumption that Indian reservations were a thing of the past. Consistent with prevailing wisdom, Members of Congress voting on the surplus land Acts believed to a man that within a short time -- within a generation at most -- the Indian tribes would enter traditional American society and the reservation system would cease to exist. Given this expectation, Congress naturally failed to be meticulous in clarifying whether a particular piece of legislation formally sliced a certain parcel of land off one reservation."

So Congress took it for granted what they were doing. But after a hundred years, what they took for granted was no longer taken for granted. Instead, what they took for granted was replaced with another special (and confusing) rule applicable to Indian law, as we'll see in the next article.

8 – THE LAW OF RESERVATIONS

There's a special law of reservations. In the last article, we saw that about a century ago, Congress passed a lot of laws diminishing or disestablishing various reservations across American. But they took for granted what they were doing, seldom explicitly saying something such as "the reservation is disestablished." Instead, they just allotted the tribal lands among the tribal members (and sometimes, too, opened the lands for settlement by non-Indians). But more lately, the fashion became to revive the old reservations. So the Supreme Court replaced what Congress simply did with another special rule for interpreting Indian law. The rule sounds sensible enough, but since the unspoken rule "the Indians always win," they've seldom lost with how the rule applied.

A leading case was Solem v Bartlett (from 1984) over the Cheyenne River Sioux Reservation in South Dakota. Back in 1908, Congress passed an act that opened 1.6 million acres for homesteading. In this case (filed near a century later), the Court ruled this act didn't "diminish" the reservation. For our purposes the facts aren't important, just the statement of the rule about the law of reservations.

The Court said, "Diminishment ... will not be lightly inferred. Our analysis of surplus land Acts requires that Congress clearly evince an 'intent . . . to change . . . boundaries' before diminishment will be found." However, "explicit language of cession ... are not prerequisites for a finding of diminishment. When events surrounding the passage of a surplus land Act ...

28

unequivocally reveal a widely held, contemporaneous understanding that the affected reservation would shrink as a result of the proposed legislation, we have been willing to infer that Congress shared the understanding that its action would diminish the reservation, ... To a lesser extent, we have also looked to events that occurred after the passage of a surplus land Act to decipher Congress' intentions."

Got that? If Congress did not explicitly say it, you look at the "events surrounding the passage," at the "widely held, contemporaneous understanding," and to "as lesser extent" at "events that occurred after the passage of" an act.

To apply this special law of reservations to the Creek Reservation, none of the many acts explicitly said the reservation disestablished. But what about the events surrounding the passage of the acts, the widely held contemporaneous understanding, or events occurring after the passage?

As we saw in the last article, Congress passed a series of acts leading to Oklahoma statehood. They allotted the tribal lands among the members and opened townsites to non-Indians. They did away with Creek tribal government. They set up a statewide legal system for Indians and non-Indians alike. They made the Creeks citizens of the new state along with everyone else. Where do you still see a reservation?

What did everyone think at the time? The Creeks thought the reservation was gone. In 1893, a Creek delegation to Washington concluded in their statement that Congress's "unwavering aim" was to "wipe out the line of political distinction between an Indian citizen and other citizens of the Republic" so that the Tribe would be "absorbed and become a part of the United States." The chief of the tribe (Pleasant Porter) in a message to the Creek Council said, "all powers over the governing even of our landed property will cease."

They were absorbed and it did cease. Upon attaining statehood in 1907, Oklahoma immediately assumed jurisdiction, including the prosecution of Indians for crimes committed on the former reservation lands. They continued to exercise such jurisdiction for over a century. Obviously, the thought never occurred they were violating the Indians' rights. Nor did the thought every occur to the Indians or the federal government. Otherwise, somebody would have said something (not to mention filed a lawsuit).

In the years afterwards, numerous federal laws referred to the *"former* reservation[s]" "in Oklahoma." After statehood, tribal leaders and members in their various messages to Congress frequently said that "there are no reservations in Oklahoma." They said the same in litigation before the federal courts. In one federal case, the Creek Tribe itself said there was only a "'checkerboard' Indian country within its *former* reservation boundaries." In several cases, the Supreme Court itself referred to the "former" lands of the Creek Nation.

No less an authority that Felix S. Cohen himself (remember, "the Blackstone of American Indian law") thought these reservations gone. In 1941, while serving as Acting Solicitor of the Interior, he wrote in a brief in a pending case that "all offenses by or against Indians" in the former Indian Territory "are subject to State laws."

But never mind. Under the unspoken rule, the Indians always win, and they won again. Since none of the acts explicitly said the Creek Reservation "disestablished," it magically reappeared. While by the same magic of legal logic, it looks like four more reservations as suddenly reappeared – the Cherokee, Chickasaw, Choctaw, and Seminole. Apparently, the eastern half of Oklahoma is once again "Indian country" (part of one or the other of these reservations).

Is Indian law hopelessly confused? It must be, since for over a century everyone had it hopelessly confused. While since four of the justices on the Supreme Court dissented, apparently they were still confused. But if you thought this case cleared up the confusion, you've got another think coming. In the next article, we'll see it only leads to more confusion.

9 – THE LAW ON RESERVATIONS

The Indians are different from you and me. They've got more legal privileges. And they've got more on the reservation than off. So since we just saw the Supreme Court re-imagine the Five Tribes' reservations (which now occupy most of eastern Oklahoma again), what legal privileges do they have on these reservations they didn't have off? But just as everyone was confused before (thinking the reservations no longer existed), they're just as confused now. We're not likely to learn the law on these reservations without further years of litigation (and since we've seen the litigation can go on for well over a century, we may never learn in our lifetime).

To start with, the Supreme Court only explicitly ruled the Creek Reservation still exists. What about the other Five Tribes' reservations (the Cherokee, Chickasaw, Choctaw, and Seminole)? By the same legal logic, they would seem to re-exist, too. But who knows for sure? Say the feds prosecute some Indian for a crime on the Cherokee Reservation (which if it still exists, the feds have jurisdiction to do). But what keeps the defense lawyers from coming up with another clever argument? Maybe they can find another technicality and argue the Cherokee Reservation doesn't re-exist after all. That seems farfetched, but then, the argument the Creek Reservation existed seemed farfetched. If everyone mistaken about the Creeks, maybe they're mistaken about the Cherokees. If so, this time around it will be the feds who have violated the defendant's rights, any conviction will have to be thrown out, and the state will have to re-prosecute the case. Who can ever know for sure until the U.S. Supreme Court hands down a decision (after years of litigation)?

As for confusing other criminal convictions (besides those of McGirt and Murphy), within weeks some 178 Indian defendants filed to throw out their Oklahoma state convictions, including 3 death penalty cases and 37 cases where defendants received a life or life without parole sentence. The Oklahoma Attorney General estimated the potential for another 1,500 to 2,000 cases. Doesn't matter how bad the crime, how guilty, or how old the case. If an Indian did the deed on the reservation, Oklahoma violated their rights (their privilege against prosecution only in federal court). The feds can refile the cases, but will all the witnesses and all the evidence still be around? Will the statute of limitations have run? Who knows?

As for confusing the day-to-day, ongoing law enforcement, the Five Tribes' rediscovered reservations cover most the eastern half of the state, 19 million acres (29,687.5 square miles) where 1.8 million people live. This population remains about 90% non-Indian and so still subject to Oklahoma laws. The state, cities, towns, and counties have to continue providing the law enforcement for all these folks. When a killing happens, an armed robbery, a rape, whatever, the local cops are still going to have to respond to the scene. But when they arrive, how do they know whether the suspect an Indian or not? If the suspect turns out an Indian (which maybe they can't determine until much later), what authority do they have to arrest, search, or question the suspect? The tribes already may have agreements cross-deputizing Oklahoma law enforcement agents. But who knows if all these agreements done right (or maybe leave some technical gaps)? Who knows if all this paperwork signed, sealed, and delivered just right? The slightest mistake along the way can easily lead to evidence or confessions suppressed and the charges dismissed (because the officers exceeded their lawful authority). Sounds like a field day for criminal lawyers.

As for what may turn out the largest confusion of all, what about all the other rights (the legal privileges) the Indians now have on these rediscovered reservations? Again, no one knows for sure, since Indian law so confused and complicated. But some thoughts must be running through the minds of lawyers anxious to make a fee by filling the litigation.

In a 1973 case (McClanahan v Arizona), a Navajo Indian living on the Navajo Reservation in Arizona protested against having to pay state income tax on earnings made on the reservation. The Supreme Court ruled as follows, "State laws generally are not applicable to tribal Indians on an Indian reservation except where Congress has expressly provided that State laws shall apply. It follows that Indians and Indian property on an Indian reservation are not subject to State taxation except by virtue of express authority conferred upon the State by act of Congress." Therefore, they ruled, "The tax is therefore unlawful as applied to reservation Indians with income derived wholly from reservation sources." Most of the City of Tulsa sits on land now part of the Creek Reservation. Then do the Indians living and working there any longer have to pay state income taxes or property taxes?

In a 1976 case (Bryan v Itasca County), the Court extended the general rule to personal property taxes. Citing the McClanahan case they wrote, "McClanahan concluded: [I]n the special area of state taxation, absent cession of jurisdiction or other federal statutes permitting it, there has been no satisfactory authority for taxing Indian reservation lands or Indian income from activities carried on within the boundaries of the reservation, and McClanahan . . . lays to rest any doubt in this respect by holding that such taxation is not permissible absent Congressional consent." They concluded the state (Minnesota this time) had no "authority in respondent county to levy a personal property tax upon petitioner's mobile home in the absence of congressional consent." Then do the Indians in Tulsa county any longer have to pay personal property taxes either?

But besides tax exemptions, Indian tribes can levy taxes on non-Indians on their reservations. In the Nebraska v Parker case (2016), the Supreme Court decided that the town of Ponder, Nebraska, was still within the Omaha Indian Reservation, although just like with the Creek Reservation, no one knew it until then. Less than 2% of the 1,600 population were tribal members. But the Court ruled the tribe could tax the businesses in the town. Since the Creek reservation now covers most of the City of Tulsa, why doesn't the same logic apply? In its *amicus curie* brief in the Supreme Court in the McGirt case, the Creek tribe argued they had the authority to tax over their whole reservation. A whole lot of non-Indian businesses are liable to find out soon whether that's right.

Doesn't this short story already show what's wrong with Indian law? First, it's hopelessly confused. You can't know what it is (without years of litigation). What everyone thought it was can suddenly turn upside down overnight, leading to only further confusion. Second, it grants Indians special rights (legal privileges) no one else has. In the next articles, let's develop the longer story in some more detail.

10 – THE INDIAN NEW DEAL

It all started with the casinos. But not really. It all started with the Indian Reorganization Act of 1934 (or the Indian New Deal). Later the casinos came along as an unexpected consequence. Then it really took off.

To go back to 1929, as a result of the Great Depression, the country wasn't in very good shape. But apparently, the Indians were already in pretty poor shape. In 1928, a government commission report (the Miriam Report, named after the author Lewis Miriam, formally *The Problem of Indian Administration*) found that, "An overwhelming majority of Indians are poor, even extremely poor ... The number of Indians who are supporting themselves through their own efforts, according to what a white man would regard as the minimum standard of health and decency, is extremely small."

Whose fault was that? Not the Indians, of course. It was the government's fault. As the report went on, "When the government adopted the policy of individual ownership of land on the reservations, the expectation was the Indians would become farmers. Part of the plan was to instruct and aid them in agriculture, but this vital part was not pressed with vigor and intelligence. It almost seems as if the government assumed that some magic in individual ownership of property would in itself prove and educational civilizing factor, but unfortunately this policy has for the most part operated in the opposite direction."

Back beginning about 1871 (when formal treaty making ended), Indian policy had become "civilization and assimilation." Just as the massive wave of foreign immigrants would pass through the American melting pot, so would these Native Americans (melding everyone). To reach this goal, which many of the Indians most ardent friends advocated as a reform, Congress passed laws doing away with tribal governments, terminating tribes, and allotting the land among the members. But apparently, giving the Indians land and turning them over to their own initiative hadn't been enough. What required was more to "instruct and aid them in agriculture." Taking the suggestion, one band of reformers pushed on down this path, trying (primarily through better education) to "civilize and assimilate" the Indians, a policy continued to about 1961.

But another band of reformers had arrived in town with Franklin D. Roosevelt on his inauguration as president in 1933. These New Dealers thought that if government had caused the problem, it also offered the solution. They didn't believe that government best which governs least. They believed in more government.

Among their number were two men immensely significant in the history of Indian law – the previously mentioned Felix S. Cohen (who served in the Solicitors Office of the Department of the Interior) and another intense advocate for the Indians, John Collier, the Commissioner of the Bureau of Indian Affairs (the BIA) from 1933 to 1945. Rather than assimilating the Indians, they wanted to revive Indian self-government. By doing so, they hoped not only to promote Indian economic development, but to preserve Indian cultures.

The Indian Reorganization Act of 1934 was their handiwork, and as far as setting up more governments, did exactly what they believed. The Act authorized the tribes to write their own constitutions, as well as form business corporation wholly owned by the tribe. Subject to approval by Secretary of the Interior, nearly all these tribal constitutions center on an elected tribal council with elected executive officers and tribal courts. At last count, some 160 tribes had constitutions set up under the IRA, with another 75 set up outside this framework. That ought to be about enough governments to satisfy anyone, but setting up new tribal governments continues apace (since to have a casino, you first need a government).

With a government, a tribe acquires "sovereignty" (the powers of government). But what powers of government do they acquire? Once again, it's complicated. In U.S. v Wheeler (1978), the Supreme Court said, "The powers of Indian tribes are, in general, *'inherent powers of a limited sovereignty which has never been extinguished.'* … Before the coming of the Europeans, the tribes were self-governing sovereign political communities. Like all sovereign bodies, they then had the inherent power to prescribe laws for their members and to punish infractions of those laws. Indian tribes are, of course, no longer 'possessed of the full attributes of sovereignty.' Their incorporation within the territory of the United States … necessarily divested them of some aspects of the sovereignty which they had previously exercised. By specific treaty provision, they yielded up other sovereign powers; by statute, in the exercise of its plenary control, Congress has removed still others."

To unpack that, then "as possessed of the full attributes of sovereignty," the tribes started out with every power a government can have (in a state of nature, all the way to life and death). And that's a "sovereignty which has never been extinguished." However, by "incorporation with the territory of the United States," these vast powers became "limited." But only to the extent "yielded up" by treaty or "removed" by a congressional law.

Then what, exactly, do they still have left over? Since there are thousands of Indian treaties and congressional laws dealing with Indians, no one can fit the pieces in this jigsaw puzzle together exactly. The "limits" on their tribal sovereignty depend on some incredibly complex rules and constantly a matter of litigation.

Just to give a quick overview at this point, tribes can't enter into direct treaties or commercial relations with foreign nations. But they're somewhat like foreign nations in relation to the states. They're semi-independent enclaves where state law only sporadically runs. For one thing, the state laws on taxation almost never run, leaving the tribes and their members in Indian country tax exempt. They've got (as seen) their own governments. The tribes and their tribal corporation have sovereign immunity (can't be sued, as some doing business with them have learned to their regret). They can exclude anyone from their land, but an exception does exist where you have a valid title to land there. They can say who a member of the tribe. They can make laws governing their land and their members. Their courts have jurisdiction over their land and can punish crimes by their members (although the punishments handed out limited by federal law). They can levy taxes, not just on tribal members, but on non-Indians doing business on their land or with the tribe.

What had Cohen and Collier wrought with the Indian Reorganization Act (the Indian New Deal)? They sure wrought a whole lot of governments with a whole lot of sovereign powers. But when it came to economic development, these governments didn't work very well. That is, not until some entrepreneur sort of Indians noticed their tribal sovereignty might let them operate casinos (when nobody else could). That's when some economic development did take off in Indian country, although spread around unevenly, mainly benefitting tribes near major centers of non-Indian population.

As for preserving Indian culture, you might persuasively argue these tribal governments didn't work very well either. What's more assimilated to the grossest aspects of

American materialism than an Indian tribe operating a casino? What's more assimilated to the grossest aspects of American political culture? If corporate America knows how to rent-seek (manipulate the political system for their benefit), the Indian tribes have thoroughly assimilated the culture.

11 – INDIAN BINGO

In 1987, the Cabazon Band of Indians had 25 enrolled members, the Morongo Band approximately 730 members. Neither may sound much of a head count for a nation, but both were "federally recognized Indian Tribes, occupy[ing] reservations in Riverside County, California." As such, both had governments. Then if we remember our Indian law from the last article, both these mini-governments had as much "inherent" power as any nation state in the world (all the "attributes of sovereignty over both their members and their territory"). As we should also remember, they could never lose a whisker of this full beard unless shaved off by a treaty or a congressional law.

Looking to make a dollar off their sovereignty (as what government doesn't), both tribes opened high stakes bingo games on their reservations, the Cabazon Band operating card games as well. Both well knew California law prohibited such gambling. That was the whole idea. As the Supreme Court would say in the case, "The games ... are played predominantly by non-Indians coming onto the reservations." The tribes were offering a diversion California (and every state in the union except Nevada) outlawed as a vice. Rather than going all the way to Reno or Las Vegas, people could now just come to the reservations, which incidentally, located in the fourth most populous county in America, close to Los Angeles and Long Beach. Come the people did like to Mecca on the hadj.

Why would the Cabazons (25 people) and the Morongos

(approximately 730 people) think themselves exempt from the laws passed by the California legislature elected by the other 28 million people in state? Of course, they thought their exemption an attribute of their sovereignty (never shaved away). They claimed to possess a legal right (a legal privilege) no one else had.

California took exception, and the usual litigation resulted with the usual result. When the case finally reached the Supreme Court (California v Cabazon Band, 1987), in a six to three decision, the Indians won again. A momentous victory it was, that would change the face of America.

But actually, California had a pretty good case. In 1953, Congress had passed a law that seemed to shave quite a few whiskers from Indian sovereignty, which brings up Public Law 280. Once again, it's complicated. With this law Congress delegated to six states jurisdiction over most crimes and many civil (non-criminal) cases throughout most of the Indian country within those states. Others states were offered an option to accept such jurisdiction, and ten states took up the offer. In other words, Congress shaved back the tribes' sovereignty, giving away these powers to the states. Yet there were a lot of gaps in this law and the courts later shaved back more. The exact borders between tribal sovereignty and state law remained a hazy (far from a bright) line.

The Cabazon Case serves as a perfect example. California was one of the six states expressly given jurisdiction over criminal cases in Indian country. To quote Public Law 280, "Each of the States . . . listed in the following table [including California] shall have jurisdiction over offenses committed by or against Indians in ... Indian country . . . to the same extent that such State . . . has jurisdiction over offenses committed elsewhere within the State ... and the criminal laws of such State . . . shall have the same force and effect within such Indian country as they have elsewhere within the State."

Indian law may be confusing, but that doesn't look confusing. Under California law, conducting such bingo and card games was a crime. It seemed clear they could enforce that law against the Cabazon and Morongo just like against everyone else ("the criminal laws of such State ... shall have the same force and effect within such Indian country as they have elsewhere within the State"). But that forgets the unspoken rule for interpreting Indian law (that the Indians always win).

A clever lawyer (sitting as a clever judge) can find a way around any law, since it's just words, and they can make the words say whatever they want (and up at the Supreme Court they speak the final word without further appeal, however much they may mangle the words). In this case, the six judge majority worked the magic by first drawing (read carefully) "a distinction between state 'criminal/prohibitory' laws and state 'civil/regulatory' laws." Next they said, "if the intent of a state law is generally to prohibit certain conduct, it falls within Pub.L. 280's grant of criminal jurisdiction, but if the state law generally permits the conduct at issue, subject to regulation, it must be classified as civil/regulatory, and Pub.L. 280 does not authorize its enforcement on an Indian reservation." And so, they managed to conclude the law against bingo and card games was a "civil/ regulatory" law, not a criminal/ prohibitory" law, so Public Law 280 gave California no authority on the reservation.

No matter how carefully you read, if that doesn't quite focus and doesn't quite make sense to the reader, it doesn't quite make sense to the author either, who has explained to the best of his ability. Gambling was a crime, punishable by a fine and jail time. Then how was that a "regulation" rather than a "criminal" law? The reader is invited to read the case personally. It's readily available over the internet. Just type in 480 U.S. 202. Good lucking making anything out of it except that the judges had a will, and they found a way. The Indians won again. The Court ruled that, "State regulation would impermissibly infringe on tribal government."

If Public Law 280 shaved something off tribal sovereignty, the tribes were amply compensated by suddenly finding an aspect of sovereignty their ancestors never knew they had. Under Canon's Canons for the interpretation of Indian law, "treaties and agreements are to be construed as the Indians would have understood them." But back at the time, none of the Indian would have conceived their treaties as granting them the right to operate casinos a century or so later. When Cohen and Collins drafted the Indian Reorganization Act of 1937 (the Indian New Deal), they wanted to revive tribal governments to promote economic development and protect Indian cultures. But they could never have conceived themselves as opening the way for the tribes to go in the casino business a half century or so later.

In the name of Indian sovereignty, the reservations were about to turn into gambling Meccas. What had before been regarded as a vice was defined down to a mere diversion. American turned into casino land. And just to notice one more thing about it, isn't this supposed to be a democracy? Well, then, millions of people had elected thousands of state legislators who had outlawed gambling in their states. But this vast majority counted for nothing. All that counted was the majority on the Supreme Court and "Indian rights."

Who said, "History repeats itself, first as tragedy and then as farce." If you regard some earlier chapters of Indian history as tragedy, how can you not regard this later chapter as farce? How could the Supreme Court keep a straight face, pretending the Indian treaties contemplated a right for them to get rich by going in the casino business (a century or so later)? Well, practice makes perfect, and Indian law has given them plenty of practice.

12 – The Indian Casinos

Why do the Indians have a right to have a casino when no one else does? We just saw the Supreme Court pop the cork on the champagne (in 1987 with the case of California v Cabazon Band). Anyone with a trace of Indian blood who didn't already have a tribe rushed to form one, and all rushed to join the party. They just didn't have a bottle, but owned the vineyard (with a surrounding legal wall, shutting out non-Indians).

It was classic rent-seeking through a legal privilege. Rent-seekers manipulate the political system for economic gain. Contrasted with profit-seeking, which adds economic value, rent-seeking merely makes a profit (at the expense of others). A legal privilege is a right that others don't have. The one easily feeds off the other, and that's exactly what happened. The tribes leveraged their legal monopoly to make a whole lot of money. At first glance, a casino might seem profit-seeking, since it does add a business of economic value (and it's definitely out to make a profit). But the Indian casinos are rent-seeking, since they expropriate the right to do business, excluding others. Just like the nobleman who put a chain across the river and expropriated the natural resource for his profit, Indian law expropriated operating a casino for the Indians at the expense of everyone else.

Fairly quickly after the Supreme Court started the party, Congress stepped in, but not to stamp out the rent-seeking, rather to stamp their imprimatur on the legal privilege. The Indian Gaming Regulatory Act of 1968 (IGRA) divided gambling into three classes. Class I were "traditional and social games played for no significant stakes and to be regulated exclusively by the tribes." Class II were "bingo [however played, with a traditional wheel or electronically], pull-tabs, lotto, tip jars" and a few card games. The tribes regulated these with approval by the National Indian Gaming Commission (NIGC). Class III were all others, "such as casino-style games, slot machines, and lotteries" (the big money makers). A tribe could only play Class III under tribal-state compacts approved by the Secretary of the Interior.

Thus, Congress threw a sop to the states. With the Class III gambling (the big money makers), the Indians have to negotiate a contract to share some of the take with the states. The states are required to negotiate in "good faith" (whatever that is). And so, although the casinos are tax exempt, the states have managed to (in effect) tax them somewhat by any other name. But as part of this deal, the states have to give the tribes the sole right to operate casinos in the state (confirming their monopoly).

Since all this started on the reservation, you might think the casinos confined to "Indian country." But since a tribe might not have any country conveniently near a big population center, a work around was devised. The Secretary of the Interior can acquire and designate land in a more favorable location as Indian "trust land." A special exception in Oklahoma lets tribes who no longer have a reservation build a casino anywhere on their former reservations. Let no facility be lacking to facilitate the gambling.

This law also set up the National Indian Gaming Commission. The president appoints their chairman and the Secretary of the Interior the two other commissioners. Their main mission is keeping the gambling fair and uncorrupted by organized crime.

The champagne has flowed and the party gone on ever

since. For 2007 through 2009, some 400 Indian casinos in 28 states churned out an annual revenue of more than $27 billion. Where does all this cash flow? To the tribes, although some of tribes don't look like much more than a party for some insiders. Many only have around a thousand members (or even fewer than a hundred). If we'll recall, the Cabazon only had 25 and the Morongo only about 730. Funding the tribal government and programs is supposed to come out of the revenue first, leaving only what left over for the per capita distributions. But with such small tribes, the government can't cost very much (the main expense probably being to run the casino), leaving over some big cash for tribal members. But you can't have everything, while the tribes' income from the casinos qualifies as tax exempt, the federal income tax applies to the per capita distributions.

Some of the money also flows into another venue – into gaming the political process. For an example, in the 1990s, the California tribes ran into a political obstacle when Governor Pete Wilson refused to include slot-machines (a real money maker) in Class III gambling. In response, in 1998, the tribes backed Proposition 5, a referendum asking the voters to approve the slot-machines. They spent $63 million compared to the opposition's $29 million and won hands down by a two-thirds majority. Other tribes have been as suitably lavish with political contributions.

So maybe all this a great thing. Maybe this one of the great things "Indian sovereignty" has brought the nation. But as for me, maybe my Puritanical streak showing. But to me, gambling not just a diversion, but a vice. If my fellow Americans disagree and want to gamble, let them do it. But rather than letting it come in the back door through the Indian tribes and their friends on the Supreme Court (who sit for life), let it come in through the proper door. Let the people in the states vote in their legislators and let their elected legislators vote in our laws. And let them vote in equal laws, applying the same to everyone, rather than rent-seeking laws, giving special legal privileges to one class of citizens over another.

13 – THE PEQUOT CASINO

"All the world's a stage, all the men and women merely players." Today, the Pequot tribe numbers a bit over a thousand. They've done very well out of playing as Indians. They don't care if you call them a farce. They're laughing all the way to the bank.

A long time ago, a Pequot tribe occupied a coastal strip in the present-day state of Connecticut. But in the early 1600s, they got wiped out in a series of wars with the English colonists. The leading historian of the Connecticut Indians, John W. De Forest, in his book (published way back in 1850) referred to them as "extinguished." That perceptive visitor to these shores, Alexis de Tocqueville, who toured the country back in 1831, mentioned them (in his *Democracy in America)* among the tribes who "now live only in men's memories." Remember the name of Captain Ahab's ship in Herman Melville's *Moby Dick* (published in 1851)? It was the Pequod, a variation of the tribal name. Melville wrote, "Pequod, you will no doubt remember, was the name of a celebrated tribe of Massachusetts Indians, now extinct as the ancient Medes."

Yet a few survived, and in the middle 1600s, the then colony of Connecticut settled this remnant on a small (about 2,000 acre) reservation. As far as anyone can piece together their later history, by 1731, about 131 people resided there, and by 1776 (the year of the American Revolution) about 151. But their numbers languished, and by 1852, they were down to 20. In 1855, the now state of Connecticut auctioned off part of the land. By 1936, the reservation was down to 128 acres with only two residents living in one dilapidated house, a lady named Elizabeth George Plouffle and a sister.

When Elizabeth died in 1973, a thoroughly American sort stepped on what now appeared an empty stage, her grandson, Richard "Skip" Hayward (born 1947). With about 1/16 Indian blood (at most) on his mother's side, it's been pointed out he could probably have better traced his ancestry back to the *Mayflower* (which carried over several Haywards) than to the Pequots. Raised mainly in Rhode Island, it's also been pointed out he wrote down for race on one of his marriage licenses – white. But whatever his race, the man was a pure born American entrepreneur.

Hayward saw some opportunity (perhaps mixed with some genuine nostalgia for his Indian heritage) in trying to re-occupy the empty stage of the small reservation. To play the Indians and the tribe, he recruited eight siblings and some 40 cousins, and they moved in, living in trailer houses financed through a HUD grant. At least it was free land, and to raise some cash for living expenses, Hayward launched them into several business ventures, including a pizza restaurant, a lettuce farm, and selling firewood.

None brought in much money at the turnstiles, so Hayward turned to some playwrights with a new script. In the 1960s, some enterprising lawyers digging through the old law books had come across a nearly forgotten law. Way back in 1793, Congress had passed what called the Non-Intercourse Act, which read, "no purchase or grant of lands … from any Indians or nation or tribe of Indians … shall be of any validity … unless the same be made by a treaty or convention entered into pursuant to the constitution." In other words, the feds were asserting their plenary (full) power over Indian affairs to the complete exclusion of the states. Congress was saying only the feds could make Indian treaties, not the states. But in the early days of the republic, several states either forgot about or simply ignored this law. Coming forward a century and a half, those former Indians lands were now home to several hundred thousand non-Indians, covered with highways, towns, houses, and businesses.

The proverbial light bulb lit up in the little balloon above the lawyers' heads. What if they could write a script for a legal resurrection? As a famous trial lawyer used to say, the angels would sing and the cash register ring. Since the law said, "no purchase or grants of lands ... shall be of any validity," any lands ceded after 1793 would still belong to the Indians. All those thousands of non-Indians would suddenly become no more than trespassers in the Indians' theater. Wouldn't matter how long they'd occupied center stage. Wouldn't matter they'd paid good money in good faith for box seats. If the lawyers could sell this new legal script to the courts, the non-Indians faced eviction (with no compensation on the way out the door). The Indians would take over the management and pay the lawyers big bucks for writing such a blockbuster hit play.

The most spectacular case involved the Passamaqquody (with today a membership around 3,500) and Penobscot (today around 2,200). They sued to recover some 6 million acres of the State of Maine (about a fourth of the state), by then home to about 350,000. The illegality of their occupation being unbeknownst to them, but was soon made known, when the federal court ruled for the Indians. However, faced with the practical (not to mention the public relations) difficulties in evicting so many people, the tribes finally agreed (in 1980, after fourteen years of litigation) to a settlement of $81.5 million.

Using the same script to stage the same play, in 1976, Hayward sued in the name of the Pequots to recover those parts of the reservation sold off by Connecticut in the middle 1800s. The defendants were the state and 35 individual landowners. But who, exactly, was the plaintiff? One of the first things you need for a lawsuit is some individual or legal entity capable of bringing it. How, exactly, was the Pequot tribe a real legal entity? But the Indians always win. The feds promptly ran up the white flag and begged for terms. In the settlement (in 1983), Hayward won two crucial things – federal recognition of the tribe and $900,000 seed money.

"The play's the thing." Now, it no longer mattered Hayward and his relatives were only play Indians. Now, only the make-believe mattered (the legal fiction, as written by the lawyers and judges). Now, the Pequots were a federally recognized tribe. Now, they had a legal right no one else had. Now, they had a right to a casino.

A Chinese Malaysian billionaire quickly came on board to produce the show, providing $60 million to build the casino (for a cut of the profits). In 1992, Foxwoods Resort Casino opened for performances. Conveniently close to huge eastern metro areas, it's been called the most successful casino in history. On any given day, about 25,000 attend the entertainment complex, which features two giant casinos, four hotels, restaurants, and several shopping centers. The slot machines alone reportedly bring in $700 million a year.

Have you ever heard a more rags-to-riches, all American success story? By playing Indians, they had gotten rich. Tribal members had free and lavish homes, free health care, free education, free just about everything. Hayward himself was pulling down $1.5 million a year as tribal chairman and as the star of the show, a high roller and big-time political player on the American stage. In the 1994 congressional elections, he wrote checks totaling nearly $500,000 to the Democratic Party and was listed among the party's "top ten supporters." During the presidency of Bill Clinton, he was several times an honored guest at the White House.

Well, perhaps this story of the Pequot casino shows Indian law at the worst. But at least when we're talking about the casinos, how can it ever get much better? How can the Indians' right to have a casino ever amount to more than a legal privilege? How can they ever disguise that cash cow under some sort of Indian regalia? It's the basest sort of rent-seeking beast, not the noble steed of an Indian warrior. Where have all the Indians gone long time passing? Like the original Pequots, they've dispersed and assimilated. They're riding the same (often ignoble) beasts as everyone else.

14 – WHO'S AN INDIAN?

Who's an Indian? Can you know one when you see one? When you see an Indian looking man on the Navajo Reservation, you're probably right he's a Navajo. Put the same guy on a busy New York City street, wearing a business suit. Few could accurately guess his ethnic origins within a thousand miles. But whether you can tell them on sight or not and depending on how you look at it, there are quite a few or not that many.

According to the 2010 U.S. Census, "Out of the total U.S. population, 2.9 million people, or .09 percent, reported being American Indian or Alaskan Native alone. In addition, 2.3 million people, or another .07 percent, reported American Indian and Alaskan Native in combination with one or more other races. Together, these two groups totaled 5.2 million people. Thus, 1.7 percent of all people in the United States." That's a lot of people, but not a very high percentage. As a footnote, while the total U.S. population grew by 9.7 percent, the Indian population grew at about double that rate. Must be a higher birthrate, more people identifying as Indian, or both.

A 1.7 percent solution not a very strong solution, but the Indians aren't entirely in solution, being spread around unevenly, often still in clusters. The Navajo, the tribe with biggest number with Indian blood alone (287,000), live heavily concentrated on their huge reservation in Arizona, New Mexico, and Utah. By contrast, the Cherokee, the tribe with the biggest overall number (819,105 in combination), live thoroughly mixed up with the general population in eastern Oklahoma and scattered far and wide beyond. Regionally, far more Indians live in the west (40.7 percent). California has the highest number and percentage (722,225 or 13.9 percent), followed by Oklahoma (482,760 or 9.2 percent). So the Cherokees must live scattered far and wide, since their numbers (819,105) nearly double the number of Indians in Oklahoma, and Oklahoma home to 38 federally recognized tribes, including the third largest, the Choctaw (195,764). As of 2020, the Bureau of Indian Affairs (BIA) legally recognized 574 tribes, but few are very big affairs. Most reported a membership in the lower thousands, many down in the hundreds or even less. The Cherokee are by far the largest number, representing some 15% of the total.

What legally makes someone an Indian? As usual, there's some confusion. *Cohen's Handbook on Federal Indian Law* says, "Who counts as an Indian for purposes of federal Indian law varies according to the legal context. There is no universally applicable definition. … there is nevertheless some practical value for legal purposes in a definition of Indian and a person meeting two qualifications: (a) that some of the individual's ancestors lived in what is now the United State before its discovery by Europeans, and (b) that the individual is recognized as an Indian by the individual's tribe or community."

So there's "no universally applicable definition," but it obviously helps if you're recognized as an Indian by a tribe. But while the Indians have a lot of rights, the right to recognition as one by a tribe isn't a right protected by federal Indian law. To quote Cohen again, "Courts have consistently recognized that one of an Indian tribe's most basic powers is the authority to determine questions of its own membership. A tribe has power to grant, deny, revoke, and qualify membership." They may require one-fourth blood, as much as one-half, or just descent from some tribal member. But they can raise the bar or decide who can't get under the bar without appeal outside the tribe.

Probably the tribes' incentives run both ways. On one hand, there's strength in numbers, and they may require more than a handful to win federal recognition (although some tribes no more than a handful). On the other hand, when it comes to the handouts (especially the casino money), the fewer hands out, the more goes in each hand. While as for the individual incentives, there's pretty much a rush on to identify as Indian and share in the handouts.

Things being what they are (with all that casino money floating around for handout), recently some instances have surfaced of tribes tightening their entrance exams or even purging the rolls. In 1995, the Pachuga Band in southern California built a casino and started paying members an annual stipend of $10,000. Enrollment applications jumped twenty-fold, resulting in the tribe putting a moratorium on new members. In 2004, with their casino profits approaching an estimated $185 million, they dropped 130 members from the rolls. In 2004, the Redding Rancheria (also in California and who also have a casino) ousted about a quarter of their members.

The most publicized conflict over membership involved the Cherokee Tribe in Oklahoma. After the Civil War, the Cherokee signed a treaty giving up their slaves and providing "persons of African descent" had "all the rights and privileges" of "native citizens" of the tribes. When Congress (around 1900) determined to allot the tribal lands, they assigned a commission (the Dawes Commission) to draw up a roll of the members. About a quarter were of African descent. Their names went on the Freedmen Rolls while the other Cherokees went on the Blood Rolls. Both received their 160 acre allotments.

But coming forward to the 1980s, the executive branch of the Cherokee government promulgated a regulation confining citizenship to members listed on the Blood Rolls. That cut out the Freedmen from voting in the tribal elections as well as from other benefits. However, in 2006, the highest Cherokee court ruled this regulation violated the Cherokee Constitution. Then in 2006, the Cherokee Council voted 13 to 2 to amend the Constitution to exclude the Freedmen. In a 2007 special election, an amendment doing just that passed by a majority of 76% (6,702) to 24% (2,041).

Since the law said the tribe can decide, the tribe looked to have decided. The Freedmen were out. But if Native Americans a cause, African-Americans are a still bigger cause. As said over and over, nothing is ever clear with Indian law. In the flurry of resulting litigation, the federal circuit court in D.C. found a way to rule for the Freedmen. Perhaps not having covered themselves with glory in this fight, the Cherokees perceived prudence the better of valor and accepted their defeat without further appeal. The Freedman are now back as citizens.

Who's an Indian? Nowadays, a lot of people are wannabes. There's "no universally applicable definition." In some later contexts, we'll see the courts have held it's a political category (legal membership in a tribe). In other contexts, we'll see they've held it's a racial category (to let Indians sue over racial discrimination). But in every context, in the end it seems a matter of blood ("some of the individual's ancestors lived in what is now the United States before its discovery by Europeans"). The Cherokee Freedmen, who don't necessarily have any Indian blood, provide an exception to prove the rule.

15 – What's an Indian Tribe?

Already a long time ago now, some of the Indian tribes took to calling themselves nations. Right now, there seems a rush on for others to change their name from such-and-such a tribe to such-and-such a nation. But there's a lot of difference between a tribe and a nation (in the sense of a nation state). Letting them confuse these two senses makes a tribe sound something more than the reality.

Cohen says, "For federal purposes, the terms 'Indian tribe' or 'Indian nation' refer to an indigenous North American group with which the United States has established a legal relationship." As for establishing the "legal relationship," a formal process exists for the Secretary of the Interior to "recognize" a tribe. As of 2020, there were 574 federally recognized tribes (231 of them in Alaska), with over 200 waiting in line for recognition (most in hope of opening a casino).

Back in 1901, the U.S. Supreme Court (in Montoya v U.S.) had these rather harsh words to say, "The North American Indians do not, and never have, constituted 'nations' as that word is used by writers upon international law, although in a great number of treaties they are designated as 'nations' as well as tribes. ... The word 'nation' as ordinarily used presupposes or implies an independence of any other sovereign power more or less absolute, an organized government, recognized officials, a system of laws, definite boundaries, and the power to enter into negotiations with other nations. These characteristics the Indians have possessed only in a limited degree, and when used in connection with the Indians, especially in their original state, we must apply to the word 'nation' a definition which indicates little more than a large tribe or a group of affiliated tribes possessing a common government, language, or racial origin, and acting, for the time being, in concert."

Not only are such harsh words never more spoken, such no longer remains good law. Today, as Cohen says, "an Indian tribe possesses, in the first instance, all the inherent powers of any sovereign state." In other words, having "all the inherent powers of any sovereign state," they're "nations." And nations have a lot of power. But he goes on to say, "inherent tribal powers are subject to qualification by treaties or by express legislation of Congress, but except as thus expressly qualified, full powers of internal sovereignty are vested in the Indian tribes and in their duly constituted organs of government." In other words, they still have all the powers of nations unless *expressly* taken away. And as we've already seen in these articles and will later see, that's still a lot of power.

No wonder they would rather call themselves nations than tribes (calling to themselves all that power). But how is calling them nations anything other than a legal fiction imposed on incongruous facts? If we take a closer look, most Indian tribes are no more than a small (and often very small) number of people with some quantum of Indian blood (often also small). Why should their blood confer on them the status of a nation state (with all that power)? We've heard of the natural man. What are they, a natural nobility? Why should their blood confer on them a whole lot of special rights (special privileges) no one else has?

To take that closer look, the census relies on self-report. How accurate is that? In the 2010 census, over 800,000 people reported some Cherokee ancestry. Perhaps that's right, or perhaps a lot of people just want to claim descent from this noble race (like former Harvard law professor and

Senator Elizabeth Warren). The Cherokee themselves report 380,000 members worldwide with 141,000 residing on or near their reservation in eastern Oklahoma. That's a pretty big discrepancy between reported ancestry and actual membership in the tribe.

Nor does the census give numbers for the 574 recognized tribes, only for some "selected tribal groupings." For example, the tribal grouping for Chippewa shows 170,742 (total, in combination with other races). But the Chippewas have divided themselves into 13 federally recognized tribes, the biggest at a bit over 40,000, the smallest around 1,500. You see the same thing for the Sioux. The census reports 170,110 (in combination). They're divided into 10 recognized tribes and report the largest as 46,855 and the smallest with only 335 members.

No completely accurate numbers appear to exist for all the 574 recognized tribes, and for some, no numbers at all. But scrounging through the available numbers, the below appears to pretty well reflect the size range for the tribes in the contiguous 48 states.

size of tribe	tribes in range
under 100 members	25
100 – 500	72
500 - 1,000	55
1,000 - 2,000	49
2,000 - 5,000	59
5,000 - 10,000	29
10,000 - 20,000	24
20,000 - 50,000	10
50,000 - 100,000	2
100,000 - 300,000	2
over 300,000	1

That's only 328 tribes, and there are 343 recognized tribes in the 48 contiguous states. The figures on the others don't appear available. While for the 231 tribes in Alaska, the available statistics are even worse. The total Native Alaskan population in Alaska reported by the census as 138,312. But no breakdown by tribes appears available.

Nevertheless, the picture that emerges appears accurate enough. Do any of the tribes fit our notion for a nation state? Possibly the Cherokees who report 380,000 members or the Navajo who report 173,667, or the Choctaw (the only other tribe reporting over 100,000). Even those are pretty small for a nation. But what can you say about the 25 tribes who report under 100 members, the 72 who report from 100 to 500, or the 55 who report from 500 to 1,000? These are nations?

Well, that's the Indian law. Those tiny blood groups are different that you and me. According to the Indian law, they're nations. They have all the power of a nation unless something expressly taken away. That's a lot of power.

Is it "one nation, indivisible," or one nation with 574 other nations living inside and off it? The tribes constantly put out statistics about how much they contribute to the economy. But all their contributions come at a rent-seeking cost to everyone else. Sure, if you give them a monopoly (like the casinos), they're going to make money that will circulate in the economy. Sure, if you give them tax exemptions (and let them tax others), they're going to have more money to circulate into the economy. But monopolies aren't efficient, and if they have a tax break, that just means someone else has to pay their share of the taxes. Why not let everyone have a casino and tax them all the same? Not only would that be fairer, it would put more money into the economy.

Seems we've got way too many nations in this country. Seems like they cost a lot more than they're worth (to anybody except them). About half the tribes in the 48 contiguous states report a membership under 2,000. Only three report a population over 100,000. These are nations?

Under Indian law, apparently so.

16 – WHAT'S INDIAN COUNTRY?

What's Indian country? Few of the boundaries are marked. Sometimes you have to research the land records and get out a surveyor. But there's a lot of it, and the feds and the tribes are continually adding more (by purchasing land and returning it to that status). The legal textbooks and commentators all say 56.2 million acres in the 48 contiguous states, the Alaskan Natives with another 44 million acres. Perhaps in more comprehensible terms, this patrimony covers 156,562.5 square miles of the earth's surface. Perhaps even more concretely, that's over one and a half times the land mass of the mother country (the United Kingdom, today England, Scotland, Wales, and Northern Ireland, altogether 93,628 square miles). That's a pretty fair chunk of ground.

The Indians are different from you and me. As Cohen tells us, "The interests that the Indians hold in real ... property represent a unique form of property right in the American legal system." You hold your real property by an ordinary title. Yours remains on the market, available to buy and sell (whether you want to sell or not). You can mortgage yours and the bank can foreclose. Your creditors can seize your house and land for non-payment of a debt. As you're very well aware, you pay property taxes plus income taxes on your income producing property. But not the Indians, who hold by an indefeasible title in perpetuity (forever) and tax exempt. Their land can never be taken away from them.

Indian country is defined by a federal statute as follows,

"[T]he term 'Indian country' ... means (a) all land within the limits of any Indian reservation ... , (b) all dependent Indian communities ... , and (c) all Indian allotments, ..."

To work through that item by item, a "reservation" means "land set aside under federal protection for the residence or use of Indian tribes" (by a treaty, a statute, or an executive order of the president). That may seem clear enough, but the boundaries have proved rather elastic. For example, in a 1993 case (Okla. Tax Comm. v Sac & Fox Nation), the Supreme Court ruled the definition included "formal and informal reservations." What's an "informal reservation," for heaven's sake (if one supposed to be designated by a treaty, a stature, or an executive order)? The Sac and Fox in Oklahoma (with a membership around 4,000, Jim Thorpe's old tribe) long ago ceded (by an 1891 treaty) all their land except an 800 acre tract, which housed the tribal government complex. Nevertheless, the Court ruled an "informal reservation" still around, which made the tribal members exempt from state income or vehicle taxes. As for the formal ones, the latest count revealed 322 federally recognized reservations, however many informal ones later litigation may reveal.

As for a "dependent Indian community," in a 1998 case (Alaska v Native Village of Venetie Tribal Government) the Supreme Court said, "[W]e have not had an occasion to interpret the term 'dependent Indian communities.' We now hold that it refers to a limited category of Indian lands that are neither reservations nor allotments, and that satisfy two requirements – first, they must have been set aside by the Federal Government for the use of the Indians as Indian land; second, they must be under federal superintendence."

As an example, the Court cited the Reno Indian Colony, which way back in 1938, the subject of another Supreme Court case (U.S. v McGowan). The Court said, "The Reno Indian Colony is composed of several hundred Indians residing on a tract of 28.38 acres of land owned by the

United States and purchased out of funds appropriated by Congress in 1916 and in 1926. The purpose of Congress in creating this colony was to provide lands for needy Indians scattered over Nevada, and to equip and supervise these Indians in establishing a permanent settlement." While never designated a reservation (by treaty, statute, or the president), yet, "The Reno Colony has been validly set apart for the use of the Indians. It is under the superintendence of the government. The government retains title to the lands, which it permits the Indians to occupy. The government has authority to enact regulations and protective laws respecting this territory." This land met both prongs of the test as a "dependent Indian community," being 1) set aside by the feds, and 2) under their superintendence.

Finally, what about the "allotments?" Such lands have been allotted from the tribal lands to tribal members, but these allotments were "restricted" (to protect the Indians from ever losing their land). They couldn't sell or mortgage their allotment (the last to prevent foreclosures). Nor could the land be seized for debt. At the same time, the land and the income from it was tax exempt. However, some ways existed to remove the restrictions, which has been done in many cases, say where the Indian owners wanted to lease for oil and gas drilling or to sell. Various procedures exist to protect the Indians from making bad deals. Nevertheless, the restrictions have been lost on much of this land. However, much has also passed down from generation to generation and still restricted. About 11 million acres remain held by individual Indians by this sort of ownership.

But Indian country is way unequally divvied up. Some tribes have got way more than others and some near none. The huge Navajo Reservation (in Arizona, New Mexico, and Utah) covers 17,544,500 acres (about 27,413 square miles). There are 12 reservations bigger than Rhode Island. But some tribes have almost none. The Reno Indian Colony mentioned above had only 28.38 acres (less than one-fifth a square mile).

How much is all this land worth? Who knows? But as Oklahoma's own Will Rogers (a member of the Cherokee tribe himself) said, "They ain't making any more of it." But with land, we always hear location, location, location. It wouldn't be worth near as much not located in the United States. They ain't making any more of it and it's in a good location. Sounds like a good long-term investment.

The Indians are different from you and me. The tribes and individual Indians hold their land by a very different title than you and me. If you would rather hold your land the same way as me, that makes good sense to me. Who wants the government standing over their shoulder and telling them what to do with their own property? But if you would rather have your land free and clear, always yours no matter what, and tax exempt besides, maybe that's not such a bad deal either.

17 – THE INDIAN EXEMPTIONS

Rather famously, Title VII of the Civil Rights Act of 1964 prohibits discrimination in employment based on "race, color, religion, sex, or national origin." American Indians qualify for this protection and have often sued and won damages. But oddly enough, the Act doesn't apply against the Indian tribes, who are specifically excluded. No one else can discriminate except the tribes, who can and do.

Originally, Indians weren't U.S. citizens, rather citizens of their tribes. But this old doctrine eroded long ago. For example, Congress made Indians citizens in Oklahoma in 1901 (before statehood). A number attended the Oklahoma Constitutional Convention, which wrote the initial state constitution, and a Chickasaw even chaired the convention. In 1924, Congress removed any doubts across the rest of the nation, passing a law which read, "The following shall be nationals and citizens of the Unites States at birth: ... a person born in the Unites States to a member of an Indian, Eskimo, Aleutian, or other aboriginal tribe."

Thus, Indians have all the rights of U.S. citizens under the U.S. Constitution, including the Bill of Rights and the 5th and 14th Amendment guarantees that neither the federal nor state governments shall "deprive any person of life, liberty, or property, without due process of law; nor deny to any person within its jurisdiction the equal protection of the laws." But again oddly enough, as our authoritative source (Cohen) tells us, "The provisions of the Constitution that constrain federal and state governments, in particular those enumerated in the Bill of Rights, do not apply to Indian tribes."

Don't let that go by without catching it. Anytime you're dealing with the feds or the states, you enjoy all your familiar legal rights as an American citizen, but not when dealing with a tribe. But two pieces of better news come right behind. First, the tribes have only limited jurisdiction over non-Indians. They don't have any criminal jurisdiction (can't charge them with a crime). As for their civil (non-criminal) laws as applied to non-Indians, it's complicated. In Indian country, the tribe may have jurisdiction, but for example, non-Indians who have a valid title to land on a reservation aren't generally subject to the tribal laws. While if non-Indians are doing business with a tribe, they may find themselves subject to the tribal laws (depends on the circumstances).

The second piece of good news is the Indian Civil Rights Act of 1968, by which Congress finally directed the tribes to start regarding most of the Bill of Rights, as well as due process and equal protection. That sounds good (and is good), but as usual with Indian law, there's a caveat. Unless the tribe actually holding you in durance vile (in custody, locked up), there's no appeal to federal court to enforce your rights. You're left to the tender mercies of the tribal courts, and instances exist where their enforcement fell far short of the federal standards. For example, in Santa Clara Pueblo v Martinez (1978) the Supreme Court let stand a tribal law that clearly discriminated against women on the ground the federal courts couldn't interfere (since nobody was locked up).

So just be aware, if you get tangled up in a tribal court, you may have far from all the protections you're used to in federal or state courts. As much as that, you're tangled up in a jurisdiction where all the players are drawn from and represent a very narrow faction (just the tribe). Their interests may vary widely from your interests, which may be bad news for you.

But beyond constitutional protections, do the ordinary federal laws apply to Indians in Indian country? Generally, yes. In Federal Power Commission v Tuscarora Indian Nation (1960) the Supreme Court stated the general rule, "that general Acts of Congress apply to Indians as well as others in the absence of a clear expression to the contrary." For example, another case (United States v Dion, in 1986) held the Endangered Species Act and Bald Eagle Protection Act applied to Indians, although the Secretary of the Interior could issue them permits for taking bald or golden eagles "for the religious purposes of Indian tribes."

However, the tribes (and their many advocates) don't like this general rule very much. They constantly claim exemptions based on their treaties and file litigation (as well as litigating against it in the academic journals). But more than that, they've won numerous exemptions from Congress and the courts.

We gave the most prominent (notorious?) example at the top. What do we hear more about than the evils of racial discrimination? Nothing. Yet the tribes have a specific exemption from the Civil Rights Act of 1964. Indians can't be racially discriminated against outside the tribe, but the tribes can (and do) racially discriminate in hiring, promotion, and salaries. Anybody else would have their socks sued off. For two other prominent examples, the tribes are also exempt from the Americans Disabilities Act of 1990 (the ADA) and the Fair Labor Standards Act (FLSA). Ramps for the disabled? The Indian tribes don't have to build them. A minimum wage and a 40-hour work week? Doesn't apply to the tribes.

For still another exemption, Indians enjoy preferential hiring and promotion to the Bureau of Indian Affairs (the BIA) and the Indian Health Service (IHS). For anyone else, such a preference would blatantly violate the accepted norms of "equal protection of the law" (as guaranteed by the U.S. Constitution). But in Morton v Mancari (1974) the

Supreme Court found a work around. In 1972, the Secretary of the Interior promulgated hiring rules for the BIA giving a preference to qualified Indians. Some non-Indian employees filed suit, claiming this denied them an equal chance for advancement. But the Court rather creativity ruled, "this preference does not constitute 'racial discrimination,' … it is an employment criterion reasonably designed to further the cause of Indian self-government and to make the BIA more responsive to the needs of its constituent groups." In a footnote, the Court added, "The preference is not directed towards a 'racial' group consisting of 'Indians'; instead, it applies only to members of 'federally recognized' tribes. … In this sense, the preference is political rather than racial in nature."

Now in the first place, since when should we want our bureaucracy staffed with civil servants "more responsive to the needs of its constituent groups?" Do we want industries and businesses (say the oil companies or the stock market) regulated more in their interests or more in the public interest? We frequently hear complaints about "bureaucratic capture," where the interests regulated by an agency capture it, running it more in their interests than the public interest. But apparently, when it comes to Indian affairs, that's exactly what the public should want.

But beyond that, in one place, the U.S. law code defines Indians as a race (when it works to their advantage). In another place, it defines them not as a race, but a political category (when that works to their advantage). Even by the roughest logic, that's a contradiction. Did we say Indian law was strange? For the Indians to win, it even contradicts itself.

18 – THE INDIAN TAX SANCTUARY

No taxation without representation?" But the Indian tribes can tax you without your representation. While as for paying taxes themselves, Indian country qualifies as a tax sanctuary.

As for the first, (Indian taxation of non-Indians), you better be careful when doing business with an Indian tribe. Some twenty-one oil companies learned that lesson the hard way from the Jicarilla Apache (a tribe with about 2,100 members and a reservation in New Mexico). Back in the 1950s, these companies signed leases to drill for oil and gas on the reservation and pay a royalty on any production (of 12½%). At the time, the tribe's constitution didn't even provide for taxing non-Indians. But by the 1960s, the thought of inserting such a proviso began to occur to a lot of tribes, and the Jicarilla promptly went along with the trend and levied a severance tax on the oil companies (6%). But hold on, the companies protested, we agreed to pay the royalty, but the leases specifically said we didn't have to agree to any further "regulations." Besides that, we're already paying a severance tax to the state (8%). But never mind. Per usual, in Merrion v. Jicarilla Apache Tribe (in 1982) the Supreme Court ruled in the tribe's favor and approved the tribal tax. Perhaps adding insult to injury, in a companion case, the Court ruled the companies had to keep paying the severance tax to the state as well (double taxation). While perhaps we should also mention, the Jicarilla are themselves exempt from paying taxes on either their royalties or their severance tax. They've got it both ways and the non-Indians got it both ways, too.

So non-Indians doing business in Indian country better not forget to write their business plan with the cost of tribal taxation in mind, remembering the tax subject to change at any time by the tribal council. If that not taxation without representation, what is it? Nobody votes for the council members except members of the tribe. The higher they tax the outsiders, the more money the insiders have. If that's not a formula for taxing to the limit, what is it? Don't forget the double taxation either (by the state as well).

As for the second (Indian country as a tax sanctuary), we've already mentioned one huge tax exemption (in an earlier article). The tribal revenue from their casinos is tax exempt. But their other tribal revenue is tax exempt as well, including as we just saw, their revenue from taxation of non-Indians doing business on the reservation. Tribes can also set up their own tribal corporations and go into business for themselves, the income tax exempt. If they need some financing, they can issue tax exempt bonds. Of course, their tribal lands are tax exempt. But taking a bit of the icing off this generous cake, they do have to pay social security and unemployment taxes on their employees.

But not just the tribes have tax exemptions, individual Indians have them. In McClanahan v Arizona (1973) the Supreme Court ruled that, "Indians and Indian property on an Indian reservation are not subject to State taxation except by virtue of express authority conferred upon the State by act of Congress. ... The [state income] tax is therefore unlawful as applied to reservation Indians with income derived wholly from reservation sources." In Moe v. Salish & Kootenai Tribes (1976) they ruled that, "the State was disabled from imposing a personal property tax on motor vehicles owned by tribal members living on the reservation, or a vendor license fee applied to a reservation Indian conducting a business for the tribe on reservation land, or a sales tax applied to on-reservation sales by

Indians to Indians." In the same term, in Bryan v. Itasca County (1976), they ruled a state lacked any authority "to levy a personal property tax upon petitioner's mobile home." Nor on their reservation lands do they have to pay for hunting or fishing licenses. Any income from their fishing is specifically tax exempt.

Indian allotments still restricted also qualify as tax exempt. By "restricted" means the allotments originally given to individual Indians and handed down so the original restrictions never removed, some 11 million acres of land. The IRS recognizes this exemption "extends to rental (including crop rentals), royalties, proceeds from the sale of natural resources of the land, income from the sale of crops grown on the land and for the use of the land for grazing purchases, and income from the sale or exchange of cattle or other livestock raised on the land." So in one field you can have a non-Indian farmer plowing away and paying every tax levied by the feds or the state. In the next field over, an Indian on an allotment can plow without such burdens.

But what about the Indian smokeshops? You may have thought they can sell at a lower price due some tax break. But for once, the Supreme Court didn't go along with the break. In Washington v. Confederated Tribes (1980), the Court said, "What the smokeshops offer these customers, and what is not available elsewhere, is solely an exemption from state taxation. ... We do not believe that principles of federal Indian law, ... authorize Indian tribes thus to market an exemption from state taxation to persons who would normally do their business elsewhere." So they ruled that sales to non-Indians weren't exempt from state taxation.

But why didn't they go with the Indians this time? As said elsewhere in the opinion, "If this assertion [that sales to non-Indians tax exempt] were accepted, the Tribes could ... open chains of discount stores at reservation borders, selling goods of all descriptions at deep discounts and drawing custom from surrounding areas." In other words, every shopping mall and big box store in America within driving distance would have relocated to Indian country. This huge tax base would have moved out of every city and town, leaving the rest of the country high and dry. The tribes could have imposed just a much lower, minimum tax. Such a tide wouldn't have raised all boats, but would have raised the tribes on a flood of revenue.

If the smokeshops have a tax break, it comes from negotiating some break with the states. Which if the states want to give them, for once it's not the fault of Indian law. You'll have to blame your state legislators for that, and you do have a vote on them.

If this tax regime doesn't qualify as a set of legal privileges, what does? If this doesn't qualify as a set of rent-seeking laws (manipulating the political system for gain), what does?

19 – INDIAN HUNTING AND FISHING

Back in the day, most Indian tribes subsisted by hunting, fishing, trapping, and gathering, although some grew crops, too. No wonder, then, since they knew no other way to subsist, virtually all the old treaties guaranteed their right to carry on this lifestyle on their reservations. When a treaty failed to say so explicitly, the courts found such rights implied. But nowadays, most Indians buy their groceries at the store. The lifestyle being gone, what about the rights? Rather frequently, those have turned into legal privileges (and frequently highly valuable ones).

In general, the states have no authority to regulate hunting and fishing on the reservations. Rather, the tribal governments have that authority and can even exclude non-Indians entirely. Some tribes have turned this into a source of substantial revenue by selling licenses to non-Indians. But cutting into the profit margin, over the years, considerable reservation land has passed into non-Indian hands, and on those lands, the state game laws can apply. But easing this pain somewhat, even when a reservation goes out of existence (partially or completely), the Indians can retain these rights over their whole former expanse. States can't require them to buy a license and can only limit their take in "exceptional circumstances" (where absolutely necessary for conservation, say to prevent the extinction of a species). To hear it from the mouth of the Supreme Court itself (in the case discussed below), "Although nontreaty fishermen might be subjected to any reasonable state fishing regulation serving any legitimate purpose, treaty fishermen are immune from all regulation save that required for conservation." We might should add, they're not limited to a subsistence level or primitive methods. They can harvest commercially and with modern methods, while as a special perk when it comes to fishing, any income qualifies as tax exempt.

A case decided by the Supreme Court in 1979 (Washington v Fishing Vessel Association) gives a good example of how such treaty rights turned into legal privileges (and highly valuable ones). This case culminated (although didn't end) decades of litigation by the tribes against Washington State. The prize at stake wasn't just some fish to fry, but the multi-million dollar industry of harvesting the anadromous fish in the Pacific Northwest. The Court tells us, "Anadromous fish hatch in fresh water, migrate to the ocean, where they are reared and reach mature size, and eventually complete their life cycle by returning to the fresh-water place of their origin to spawn. … The regular habits of these fish make their 'runs' predictable; … the management of anadromous fisheries is in many ways more akin to the cultivation of 'crops' -- with its relatively high degree of predictability and productive stability."

For centuries, these fish were a large source of food for the tribes in the Pacific Northwest. When in the 1850s, they agreed to move onto reservations, their treaties guaranteed them access to their traditional fishing grounds (both on and off their reservations). The treaty with the Yakima tribe was typical, reading, "[t]he exclusive right of taking fish in all the streams, where running through or bordering said reservation, is further secured to said confederated tribes and bands of Indians, as also the right of taking fish at all usual and accustomed places, in common with citizens of the Territory." In other words, they got an exclusive right on the reservations, but off the reservations only a right "in common with the citizens of the Territory."

No problem at the time, since as the Court tells us, "At the time the treaties were executed, there was a great abundance of fish and a relative scarcity of people." But fast forward a century and the numbers reverse. The fish are scarce relative to the abundance of people. "Millions ... are harvested each year. Over 6,600 nontreaty fishermen and about 800 Indians make their livelihood by commercial fishing." Modern methods let them catch virtually every fish going upriver. To prevent over-fishing to eventual extinction, the State of Washington passed some laws to manage the resource by limiting the catch.

But the Yakima and a whole host of other tribes objected. They "contended that the treaties had reserved a preexisting right to as many fish as their commercial and subsistence needs dictated." More bluntly put, Washington had no right to limit their catch in any way, apparently, even to extinction.

As usual, the Indians won, but while they won a big slice of the pie, this time not the whole cake. The Supreme Court ruled that Washington could limit the overall catch for conservation (to prevent extinction). But whatever the limit decided on, the Indians were entitled to between 45% and 50% of the harvest. In other words, the tribes won a partial (and extremely lucrative) monopoly. The 800 Indian commercial fishermen split about half the profits, leaving the 6,600 non-Indians to divvy up the leftovers.

How did the Court arrive at this formula? Creatively, since the treaties never mentioned or contemplated any such thing. Once again, the opinion relied on Cohen's Canons of privileged interpretation. The Court said, "[T]he treaty must therefore be construed, not according to the technical meaning of its words to learned lawyers, but in the sense in which they would naturally be understood by the Indians." But hold on a minute. How could even the Indians (back at the time) have understood the treaties as the Court just construed the words?

Look back at the exact words. "[T]he exclusive right of taking fish in all the streams, where running through or bordering said reservation, is further secured to said confederated tribes and bands of Indians, as also the right of taking fish at all usual and accustomed places, in common with citizens of the Territory."

Back at the time, how could the Indians have understood these words to say their catch could never be limited? Such a thought never entered their minds, since at the time, the fish looked an inexhaustible resource. How could they have understood these words to apply to commercial fishing? Such a thought was not in their minds, since fishing to them meant fishing for food, not to make a profit. How could they have understood these words gave them more rights to fish off the reservation than anyone else? The words said, "in common with citizens of the Territory."

No, once again, it's the unspoken rule. The Indians always win. Under that rule, their hunting and fishing "rights" turned into a very pleasant and valuable "legal privilege." They can hunt and fish over vast stretches of America with no license and no limit. Out in the Pacific Northwest, they get about half the profit from the commercial fishing. Their income from the fishing is tax exempt. Not a bad interpretation for something that never entered their minds at the time.

20 – INDIAN CRIMES

Being prosecuted in a special court was an old-time privilege. Remember benefit of clergy? Way back in the Middle Ages, you couldn't prosecute a priest in the ordinary courts. They had their own special courts (the ecclesiastical courts). Since staffed wholly by the clergy, they might expect some special treatment. But they weren't the only ones. In England, you couldn't prosecute a nobleman in the ordinary courts either. They had a right to a trial before the House of Lords, where again, since staffed wholly with the nobility, they might expect some special treatment.

Eventually, England did away with such special courts. But the memory provides one reason behind our American legal maxim – "equal protection of the laws." We wanted out laws to treat people equal.

But as we saw in the McGirt and Murphy cases, this old-time privilege lingers around in perhaps a surprising form. Indians have a special right against prosecution in the state courts. It's complicated like the rest of Indian law. But often only the federal or tribal courts can prosecute them. If they might not expect any special treatment there, yet we've seen them manage to leverage this special status to their advantage, as McGirt and Murphy did. They got their twenty-year old convictions thrown out and new trials, while since there's no death penalty for Indian crimes, Murphy can at least avoid that fate this time around.

What exactly, does this legal privilege amount to? Back at the start, neither federal nor state law ran in Indian country, only tribal law. However, way back in 1817, concerned with protecting the Indians from the "lawless whites on the frontier," Congress passed the Indian Country Crimes Act (ICCA). That extended the federal criminal laws against non-Indians in Indian country, but specifically said, "shall not extend to offenses committed by one Indian against the person or property of another Indian." So in an old case still in the law books (Ex Parte Crow Dog, from 1883), a Sioux chief named Crow Dog killed another Sioux chief named Spotted Tail. A federal court sentenced him to hang. But the Supreme Court vacated the conviction. Since the crime was by one Indian against another in Indian country, only Sioux tribal law applied. Fortunately for Chief Crow Dog, that provided not for hanging, but only the payment of restitution.

This case led Congress to pass the Major Crimes Act in 1885 (the MCA), saying, "Any Indian who commits against the person or property of another Indian or other person any of the following offenses, [and it gives a list of major crime] within the Indian country shall be subject to the same law and penalties as all other persons committing any of the above offenses." In others words, now "Indians" who committed one of these crimes (against anyone) could be prosecuted in the federal courts. On this list (of major crimes) were "murder, manslaughter, kidnapping, maiming, incest, … felony child abuse or neglect, arson, burglary, robbery." But it was far from a complete list. However, the Assimilative Crimes Act (the ACA, passed back in 1825) appears to have filled in most of the gaps. If an Indian commits a crime not on the list in the Major Crimes Act, they can be prosecuted (but still only in federal court) under the provisions of the criminal code of the state where the crime occurred.

Coming down to the present day, mainly through decisions of the Supreme Court, the following sums up criminal jurisdiction in Indian country. 1) The states can prosecute non-Indians who commit crimes against non-Indians 2) Only the feds can prosecute non-Indians for crimes against Indians. 3) Only the feds can prosecute Indian crimes against non-Indians, unless the perpetrator already punished by the tribe. 4) The feds can prosecute Indians for crimes against other Indians listed in the Major Crimes Act, but otherwise the tribal courts have exclusive jurisdiction. While as for the tribal courts, federal law limits the punishments to three years of incarceration per offense and/or a $15,000 fine and no more than nine years incarceration per criminal proceeding.

If you're somewhat confused at this point, you're not the only one. It's been called a "jurisdictional maze" or a "crazy quilt." You need a chart to figure out who fits where. But before you can figure out which court, you have to figure out the who and the where. Is the suspect an Indian? Complicated rules exist as to who qualifies. Did the crime take place in Indian country? Since Indian country often consists of parcels of land scattered around a state in a checkerboard fashion, you may have to research the land records and call out a surveyor.

But there's an exception to all this. By Public Law 280 (passed in 1953) Congress gave six states jurisdiction to prosecute most crimes throughout Indian country within their borders (no matter who committed them). The others states were given an option to assume such jurisdiction. Ten opted to do so, although some only assumed a partial jurisdiction. To sort it out, you have to go state by state

If such not complex enough to leave a bunch of legal loopholes to go through in court, all these competing jurisdictions give law enforcement out in the field endless problems. An officer who makes a mistake and acts outside his jurisdiction has no legal authority to act. As a result, any confession he may take or evidence he may seizes ends up "suppressed" (thrown out and can't be used to convict).

For one example, take State v Yazzie (a 1989 case out of New Mexico). The Court said, "It is undisputed that a San Juan County Sheriff Department detective obtained an arrest warrant for defendant's arrest from a state magistrate. San Juan County deputy sheriffs Trotter and Vaughn went onto the Navajo reservation to locate defendant. They requested the assistance of the Navajo Tribal Police in the arrest, but were informed that a tribal policeman would not be available for three hours. The officers were concerned that vital evidence (the murder weapon) might disappear and would be lost based on information they had. In light of this concern, they proceeded to arrest defendant at his home on the reservation without the assistance of a tribal policeman."

The Court then lowered the boom on such illegal conduct (no, not on the part of the murder suspect, on the part of the offices). The judge ruled, "under the tribal code, only tribal policemen are authorized to carry out an on-reservation arrest of an Indian. Since the on-reservation arrest in the present case was not carried out by a tribal policeman ... the arrest was illegal." And so, the "defendant's on-reservation arrest was invalid." Any evidence the officers seized was suppressed and couldn't be used to convict. The Court further noted, "The misconduct in this case was committed by the state officials," perhaps forgetting any misconduct the suspect may have committed in committing a murder.

"Equal justice under law." That's the motto the U.S. Supreme Court has up on the façade of their building. How does the Indian criminal law serve such a motto? Indians have their own special courts and their own special loopholes. How is that equal?

21 – THE INDIAN STEP-FATHER

If the feds the Great Father, the states play the role of the unloved step-father. And frankly, there's not much love lost either way. The tribes don't want anything to do with the states except to live off them. The states are tired of the tribes, who while proclaiming themselves as grownups (and wanting to govern themselves), still want to live cost-free in the family house.

What about the Indian law causes such hard feelings? Way back in 1831, Chief Justice Marshall wrote in the famous case of Cherokee Nation v Georgia, "The Cherokee Nation ... is a distinct community ... in which the laws of Georgia can have no force ... but with the assent of the Cherokees themselves, or in conformity with treaties, and with acts of Congress." All these years later, that's still good law with respect to all the federally recognized tribes.

To sort that out precisely, 1) the laws of a state have no force against an Indian tribe, unless, 2) the tribe assents (not likely), 3) a treaty so provides, or 4) Congress so provides with a law. But to apply these four simple looking rules to, 1) all the 574 recognized tribes, 2) in all 50 states, 3) as provided by all the thousands of treaties, statutes, and court decisions, 4) multiplies the complexity and confusion to a never-ending number. At least, the litigation has been never-ending.

Now, under Cohen's Canons of Construction, a state asserting some jurisdiction over a tribe based on a treaty or statute starts out behind the eight ball (with the presumption against them). Recall that, "The basic Indian law canons of construction require that treaties, agreements, statutes, and executive orders be liberally construed in favor of the Indians, and that all ambiguities be resolved in their favor." Not surprising, then, the states have routinely lost the cases where they sought to assert some jurisdiction.

To go through some examples by the numbers, 1) The tribes have sovereign immunity. The state courts have no jurisdiction over them (and we might add, neither do the federal courts). In Kiowa Tribe v Manufacturing Technologies (1998), the Supreme Court stated, "an Indian tribe is subject to suit only where Congress has authorized the suit or the tribe has waived its immunity." And that's even when the "contracts involve governmental or commercial activities and whether they were made on or off the reservation."

In the case itself, a non-Indian corporation learned this lesson the hard way. The facts showed that, "the Kiowa Industrial Development Commission agreed to buy from … Manufacturing Technologies certain stock … the then-chairman of the Tribe's business committee signed a promissory note in the name of the tribe. By its note, the Tribe agreed to pay … $285,000 plus interest … the Tribe executed and delivered the note … in Oklahoma City, beyond the Tribe's lands, and the note obligated the Tribe to makes its payments in Oklahoma City." But the tribe defaulted, and Manufacturing Technologies sued. Too bad for them. The tribe's sovereign immunity blocked the suit. However, three justices did dissent, saying, "Governments, like individuals, should pay their debts and should be held accountable for their unlawful, injurious conduct." But tribal sovereign immunity looks safe for now.

2) You also better beware doing business with Indians on the reservation. The state courts may have no jurisdiction there. In Williams v Lee (1959) a non-Indian operated a trading post on the Navajo Reservation. When

one of his Navajo customers failed to pay, he sued in the state courts. But no luck. The Supreme Court ruled, "No Federal Act has given state courts jurisdiction over such controversies. ... There can be no doubt that to allow the exercise of state jurisdiction ... would infringe on the right of the Indians to govern themselves." That left the trading post owner to try his luck in the tribal courts, but we're not told how that came out.

To go on by the numbers, we've already seen a number of other examples. 3) The tribes and tribal businesses are exempt for state taxation. That's in or out of Indian country, but for individual Indians, the following only apply while in Indian country. 4) They're exempt from state income taxes. 5) They're exempt from state real property taxes. 6) They're exempt from state personal property taxes. 7) They're exempt from state motor vehicle taxes or vendor license fees. 8) They're exempt from state hunting and fishing regulations or fees.

But there's the exception to prove the rule (as always with the law). In Washington v Confederated Tribes (1980), the Supreme Court held states could tax retail sales to non-Indians even in Indian country. The case itself involved cigarette sales, but the principle applies to any retail sales. Otherwise, the tribes could in effect market their tax exemption. By levying a much lower tribal tax, they could clean up by making their reservations into entrepots for shopping malls and big box stores, sucking that huge tax base away from the states.

We can easily understand why the tribes don't love the states. Who wants to be under any law at all? And they've fought free from virtually all state laws. We can as easily understand why the states don't love the tribes. Many a state politician may screw up his face and say nice things out on the stump. After all, Indians vote, too, and nowadays, many a tribe wields a heavy political stick through routing some of their gambling revenue into campaign contributions. But when those same state politicians reach for their wallets and start counting their money, nice thoughts are less likely to come to mind. A man's heart may not be in his wallet, but besides their love for getting elected, state politicians don't regard much more fondly than their state budgets. To keep getting elected, they have to bring home the bacon and the bacon in their budgets. Coming to pour over those balance sheets (and the items of revenue and expense), they can't help but notice the tribes are all outgo and no income. The Indians are living on the state budget just like everyone else. They're driving the state highways, attending the state schools, and have as much as anyone else from the state. But the tribes, their land, and their income are off the tax rolls (although the state may get a little something from those revenue sharing compacts on the casinos).

No, there's no love lost between the tribes and the states. The Indians always win, and the states are tired of losing to them (in federal court). But what they're most tired of losing is the tax income. And isn't that a genuine grievance? They're forced to house the tribes, but the tribes live cost-free in the house.

22 – THE INDIAN RESOURCES

Becalmed on the ocean with the water casks empty, the Ancient Mariner looked out and saw, "Water, water everywhere, but not a drop to drink." But looking out across the American west, we don't see water everywhere and not everyone can drink. Water is a precious commodity and who gets to drink a matter of contention. Why should anyone express surprise the Indians drink first and as much as they want? And that's just one example of their preferential status to natural resources.

When just over two million people (the actual membership in the tribes) sitting on some 156,562.5 square miles of the earth's surface (one and a half times the land mass of the UK, which carries a population of 68 million), they're sitting on a huge mass of natural resources as well. But to stay with the water in the American west for a moment, in a 1973 case (Colorado River Water Conservation District), the Supreme Court said, "It is probable that no problem of the Southwest section of the Nation is more critical than that of scarcity of water. As southwestern populations have grown, conflicting claims to this scarce resource have increased."

So who gets what? To adjudicate these conflicting claims over the critical scarcity of water, the western states follow what called the "doctrine of prior appropriation." The Court went on to state this doctrine as follows, "Colorado applies the doctrine of prior appropriation in establishing rights to the use of water. Under that doctrine, one acquires a right to water by diverting it from its natural source and applying it to some beneficial use. Continued beneficial use of the water is required in order to maintain the right. In periods of shortage, priority among confirmed rights is determined according to the date of initial diversion." In other words, as has been said, "First in time, first in right."

But of course, the Indians have their own special rights called "the reserved rights doctrine." Under this doctrine, creating a reservation automatically "reserves" the needed water rights. That sure makes sense. How can you live on a reservation without water? But the doctrine doesn't stop there. Unlike non-Indians, they don't have to put the water to some beneficial use or continue to use it. It's simply reserved for them for all time. And not just the water needed when the reservation created, rather, any water they might need at any future time. As the Court said in another case (Arizona v California, in 1963), "the water was intended to satisfy the future as well as present needs of the Indian Reservations." While since virtually all reservations created prior to any appropriation of water by non-Indians, the Indian water rights virtually always come before anyone else's. As the practical result, they drink first and all they need. If your crops wither while their crops flourish, that's just another of their legal privileges. On the other hand, since they might have more water reserved (for future use) than needed right now, they might be willing to sell you some.

As for other Indian resources, outside Alaska those 156,562.5 square miles are mostly grasslands (77%), which suitable for raising livestock. Back in 2006, this generated an income of approximately $550 million. Another about 11,500 square miles are forests suitable for harvesting timber. As for the underground, the tribes are the third largest owners of oil and gas reserves (3 to 4%), have 30% of the coal west of the Mississippi, and 40% of all the uranium.

In the past and still, the feds have leased out these resources for the tribes, although increasingly, the tribal governments are taking over and doing it for themselves. The feds should be glad to leave this responsibility behind, since when they do it, they act as "trustees" for the tribes. A trustee must perform to a fiduciary standard, the highest standard imposed by the law. In Seminole Nation v. U. S. (1942), the Court said, "In carrying out its treaty obligations with the Indian tribes, the Government ... has charged itself with moral obligations of the highest responsibility and trust. Its conduct ... the acts of those who represent it in dealings with the Indians, should therefore be judged by the most exacting fiduciary standards."

Things being what they are, the Indians' lawyers have rather often convinced the courts that the feds failed to come up to such a high standard. The law books are full of cases where the tribes won significant damages. Their most spectacular win came in the Cobell Case (filed in 1996), which concerned the Individual Indian Money (IIM) Accounts.

As mentioned several times, back beginning in 1887, a great deal of tribal land was allotted to individual Indians. We're talking about hundreds of thousands of allotments. The U.S. government (and specifically the Department of the Interior) acted as a trustee for all the thousands of Indians entitled to the income from the land (such as from farming and grazing leases or oil and gas leases), responsible for receiving and paying it over to them. These were called the Individual Indian Money (IIM) Accounts. But over the years, this program turned into an administrative nightmare. An Indian would die, dividing his or her share among their heirs. Their heirs would die, further dividing the shares. Somewhere along the way, the Interior Department began to lose track. And no wonder. During the course of the lawsuit, it was estimated there were 1.4 million fractional interests subdividing 58,000 tracts of land. Nobody was embezzling any money, but Interior simply wasn't able to keep up. How did they known when an Indian died or who were their heirs? At any rate, they failed to pay a lot of money over to a lot of Indians who were due it (although nobody could ever figure out how much or which Indians). At any rate, the federal courts found this breached the government's fiduciary duty to the Indians.

In 2010, the litigation settled for $1.5 billion to be paid over to some 300,000 individual Indians. That left the problem of determining exactly who they were, but as of 2011, some 263,500 Indian claimants had been mailed their checks. Another $1.9 billion was set aside to buy back fractional interests from individual Indians and return that land to the tribe (and some 1.7 million acres have been returned). Last but not least, the Indians' lawyers were paid $99 million (did we mention the Indian law a nice revenue stream for the lawyers).

23 – THE INDIAN BUREAUCRACY

The Indians are different than you and me. They've got their own federal programs, their own federal bureaucracies (which as seen, staffed by them), and their own federal funding. More than that, the tribes now have their own tribal bureaucracies with their own federal funding. After all, they're governments, aren't they? What's a government without its own bureaucracy?

Perhaps the Indian Health Service (IHS) provides the best example. Universal health care? The Indians already have it. The IHS provides free health care to members of federally recognized tribes, but formal enrollment not required, only Indian descent and some affiliation with an Indian community. Fully funded by the feds, the agency serves all 574 federally recognized tribes in 37 states, approximately 2.56 million Indians. With a staff of over 15,000, the IHS operates 46 hospitals as well as numerous other health care facilities. The budget in 2020 was $6 billion.

But while the IHS an agency funded by Congress, Indian tribal bureaucracies actually administer over 60% of the program (and the appropriations). How does that work? The Indian Self-Determination and Education Assistance Act (1975) "devolved" the federal authority to the tribes. This law let them enter into "contracts" with federal agencies to take over and run their federal programs for themselves. Today, not only do they run 60% of the IHS, they run about half of the other federal Indian programs. But if you're going to administer a government program, you need a bureaucracy to do it. So under this law, the feds also pay for the tribal bureaucracies (pay what called the "contract support costs").

To come back to these "contracts" in a moment (and the associated "contract support costs"), besides health care, what are some other major federal programs for Indians? The feds fund Indian elementary and secondary schools (some 183 schools in 23 states with 47,000 students) and tribally controlled colleges (some 33 colleges). They provide higher education grants (for Indians to attend institutions of higher education). They fund Indian social programs, including welfare and child welfare. They fund roads and bridges in Indian country (some 29,000 miles of roads and 900 bridges). They fund dams, irrigation systems, and water systems. They fund Indian housing. They fund Indian law enforcement. What about Indian government don't they fund?

Any complete list would fill a book, and does fill what amounts to several books in the *Federal Register*, where all the bureaucratic regulations written down. While in addition, of course, Indians are served by all the other federal programs listed in that book (the same as any other citizen) as well as any state programs. The land of the free and the brave? Nowadays, it's also the land of entitlements, and you can't accuse the Indians of not getting their share, although they (like everyone else) still want more.

How many layers of bureaucracy can you have? Never enough to satisfy the bureaucrats. The lawyers love to multiply the legal complexity because you have to hire them to guide you through the labyrinth or show you where to hide out in the corridors. Bureaucrats love to multiply the complexity because they love a large vista where they're lost in the view. The bigger the bureaucratic maze, the bigger their domain and the harder to locate them in it (to fix their accountability and hold them responsible). The tribal bureaucracies fit well with this preferred design, adding still another highly opaque layer.

The Indians always win, and there's a case about tribal bureaucracy that proves the maxim once again. In Salazar v. Ramah Navajo Chapter (decided by the Supreme Court in 2012), the facts were as follows. As said, an Indian tribe can enter into a "contract" to manage a federal program for itself. Under the law, the feds can only refuse such a contract if they can "clearly demonstrate" some valid reason. Also, the feds have "to pay the "full amount" of "contract support costs" (that is, what it costs the Indian bureaucracy to run the program). But, "The Act also provides, however, that … the provision of funds … is subject to the availability of appropriations." In other words, Congress didn't intend the program as a blank check. Rather, the check was only good up to the amount that Congress appropriated.

As the law fairly peremptorily directed him to do, the Secretary of the Interior (the official with the authority to sign for the government) entered into such contracts with a number of tribes. As peremptorily directed, these contracts provided the government would pay the "full amount" of the contract costs. But then Congress didn't appropriate enough money to cover all the costs as submitted by the tribes. Left without sufficient funds to pay them all, the Secretary divided the available money on a pro rata basis among them.

Not good enough for the tribes, who whatever they win from Congress (and they've won quite a lot), are very well aware they can almost always win more through the federal courts. And lo and behold, after this particular litigation ran on for some twenty years, they did win again. The Supreme Court found a way to pay them. Figure it out if you can. When Congress says the payments are "subject to the availability of appropriations" and then appropriates only so much money, how do you get around that (logically)? But we've already seen that when the judges have a will, they have a way. Once again, the Supreme Court found a way to rule for the Indians (although only by a bare majority with four justices dissenting).

How much did the tribes win? The case settled for close to a billion dollars ($940 million). Knowing when it was whipped, Congress appropriated the money.

24 – THE INDIAN FRONTIER

The historian Frederick Jackson Turner (1861 to 1932) achieved fame with his "frontier thesis." He proposed life on the rather lawless American frontier formed a distinctive American character. But the frontier closed down around 1890, and as part of that frontier, the old, wild Indian tribes closed down about the same time. But by today, the tribes have found their way to a new frontier – the frontier of Indian sovereignty.

A distinguished commentator on international law writes, "Sovereignty is a bad word, ... it is often a catchword, a substitute for thinking and precision. It means many things, some essential, some insignificant; some agreed, some controversial ... . For legal purposes at least, we might do well to relegate the term sovereignty to the shelf of history as a relic from an earlier era." But the commentators on Indian law and the Indian tribes couldn't disagree more. They love the word. *SOVEREIGNTY*. No word is more sacred in their mouths. And why? Precisely because it's "a catchword, a substitute for thinking and precision."

Take that oft quoted and authoritative source, *Cohen's Handbook on Federal Indian Law*, "Indian tribes consistently have been recognized ... as 'distinct, independent political communities,' qualified to exercise powers of self-government, ... by reason of their original tribal sovereignty. ... Once recognized ... by the United States, a tribe retains its sovereignty until Congress acts to divest that sovereignty. Perhaps the most basic principle of all Indian law … is that those powers vested in an Indian nation [are] … inherent powers of a limited sovereignty which has never been extinguished."

That uses the word "sovereignty" four times (in speaking about the Indian tribes "powers of self-government"), but where do you see any precise thinking about the word? The tribes are "qualified to exercise powers of self-government" by their "sovereignty." But what precisely are those "powers?" "It all depends on what the definition of is is." It all depends on what the definition of sovereignty is. But no definition is given.

Can you look somewhere else then (for some thinking and precision)? You can read the close to 1,500 pages of *Cohen's Handbook* and as many of the hundreds of court cases cited as you can manage. But after all that toil, you'll seldom know "Indian sovereignty" when you see it. As these articles show, what you might think you know will often turn out wrong (and suddenly turn upside down). What you think you know often just leads to further confusion. You'll seldom come to know it upfront, but only after-the-fact (after years of litigation).

Recall some examples of their sovereign powers no one knew about upfront (only after-the-fact). No one knew about their sovereign power to have a casino (until after the Cabazon Case, in 1987). No one knew the Five Tribes' sovereign powers still existed across their reservations (until the McGirt Case rediscovered the reservations, in 2020). No one knew the tribes' sovereign powers let them tax non-Indians on the reservation (until Merrion v. Jicarilla Apache Tribe, in 1982). No one knew the tribes' sovereign powers exempted Indians on the reservation from state taxation (until a whole series of cases). No one knew the sovereign powers of the tribes in the Pacific Northwest entitled them to about 50% of the anadromous fish (until Washington v Fishing Vessel Association, in 1979).

So gentlemen, file your lawsuits on this new Indian

frontier. Stake a claim to your Indian sovereignty and see if you can't make good your title. You never know for sure (upfront), and the wildest claims often win (after-the-fact). You never know whether a claim to Indian sovereignty is good or not until the Supreme Court stamps the deed (which they seem eager enough to do). While approving one claim just leads to the filing of further claims for further sovereignty.

Frederick Jackson Turner's frontier may be gone, the Wild West may be gone with it, but not this modern-day legal frontier of Indian sovereignty. The line of settlement (marked by the tribe's sovereign powers) constantly advances, but the frontier still stretches to the horizon. New tribes in the hundreds are clamoring for recognition of their sovereignty. The feds are buying up land and restoring it to the tribes, restoring their sovereignty. The tribes themselves are buying up land, extending their sovereignty. New sovereign powers are constantly discovered. It's a restless and moving frontier.

For one further suggestion to push on the line of settlement, Cohen tell us, "[B]oth [a] U.N. Draft Declaration and the Proposed American Declaration [proposed by the Organization of American States (the OAS), not the U.S. states, but nation states across both North and South America] recognize a right of indigenous peoples to the 'restitution for the lands, territories, and resources which they have traditionally owned or otherwise occupied and used, and which have been confiscated, taken, occupied, used, or damaged.' While this right is not absolute, it suggests the emergence of an international norm requiring the restoration of indigenous lands on a scale much larger than obtained by Native Americans to date."

In other words, The American Indian tribes' sovereignty already stretches over an area more than one and a half times the size of the UK. But an "international norm" now suggests the "restoration of lands on a scale much larger," stretching their sovereignty still further. What "scale" would that be? What percentage of the land does 1.7% of the population need to own (as "restitution," forever and tax free)?

What is sovereignty? The word that keeps recurring in the definition is "power." Sovereignty is government power. But it's an imprecise word (which exactly why the Indian tribes and their lawyers love it). By constantly expanding the definition with more powers, they can constantly advance the frontier of Indian sovereignty. If they can't have it all (can't have full sovereign powers), they want as much as they can get (with no end in sight).

Indian sovereignty has become a talisman. Indian sovereignty has become the genie in the lamp. Rub the word and power comes out. Rub the word and special legal privileges come out. No wonder the tribes love the word.

25 – THE END OF INDIAN LAW

The Indians are different from you and me? Not really. The only difference is they've got more legal privileges. But why should that be?

"A man's a man for a' that and a' that." What makes Indians different from you and me (what's the "a' that")? Nothing except their legal privileges (their rights no one else has). Let them and their many friends look in the mirror. What else do they want to call the face looking back at them (if not their legal privileges)? Let them rationalize all they want. Let them talk (all they want) about their historical grievances. Let them talk (all they want) about preserving their native cultures. Let them talk (all they want) about their sovereignty. When the talking over, nothing is staring back at them in the mirror except their naked self-interest (a power lust, not wearing enough clothes to fool the innocence of a child). Either that, or the aphrodisiac of power has addled their brains until they can't recognize themselves in the mirror. There's a move on to preserve and revive the Indian languages. In any language, all their rationalizations translate into just one word – power. It's all about the power (the legal privileges other people don't have).

They're no different than you and me. If we look in the mirror, we'll see the same image staring back at us (our self-interest). They just saw a chance to take some advantage and took it. Who can blame them? We're no better. We've taken enough advantage in our time. But it's time to stop taking advantage of each other. "All men are created equal." Let's start living by the motto.

A distinguished philosopher has said, "The history of the world is full of peoples, tribes, classes, nations, etc., who cheat by claiming a right to special privilege, and nothing I say will stop some people from cheating." How right he was. "All men are created equal." What does that mean? All men are created equally inclined to cheat? Maybe so. But mankind has a better side. The "rule of law" was meant to stop the cheating.

The rule of law refracts our self-image (correcting for the self-interested flaw in our vision). With the rule of law, we're forced to look through three sights simultaneously, 1) clearly stated laws, 2) clear and fair legal procedures, and 3) equal protection of the laws. When all three line up, we see a better image in the mirror.

But Indian law sets its sights on another target – preferences and privileges for the Indians. Clearly stated laws? Indian law consists of a confused mass (thousands) of treaties, statutes, executive orders, bureaucratic regulations, and court decisions. Sighting along Cohen's Canons of Construction (which give every preference to an interpretation most favorable to the Indians), a clever lawyer can almost never fail to find and hit the target (still more legal privileges for the Indians) in such a confused and massive body of law.

Clear and fair procedures? Yes, the federal courts reliably hit this target. But what about the tribal courts? They follow their own tribal constitutions, and so all the familiar "due process" protections in the U.S. Constitution don't necessarily apply. But as much as that, the federal courts rest on a very broad base (as broad as the nation). No one's an outsider (not even the Indians, who can hardly complain about their treatment there). But the tribal courts rest on a narrow base (sometimes no more than a few thousand). They're the insiders and everyone else the outsiders (since no one else a citizen of the tribe). Oh, they say they'll be fair. Why should we ever doubt their word? But when did we ever see them interpret a law so as not to give themselves every advantage (against outsiders)? In their courts, you can reliably expect them to hit that target.

Equal protection of the laws? With the Indian law, the rest of us go around with targets on our backs. All their special rights and privileges come at a rent-seeking cost to everyone else. Since that's all they're aiming at, that's all they can ever hope to hit. The Indians always win, and we always lose.

But why should that be? Why should the Indians be different from you and me (have all these legal privileges)? They shouldn't. We should all live by the rule of law.

Then if this cure sounds radical, so is the disease. And there's no other cure except for the Indians privileges to die on the operating table. If that sounds painful to them, yet the Indians won't die. After the surgery, they'll be no worse off than the rest of us (still have all the rights anyone else has). If that's not sufficient consolation, they'll still have all the property they had before the operation. The 5th Amendment says no one's property can be taken "without just compensation." Nor can theirs. Nor should anyone suggest such a thing. All they'll lose are their special legal privileges.

The casinos? Convert them into ordinary corporations with the tribal members as the shareholders. Let them compete like everyone else (without a monopoly). Being first out the gate should be competitive advantage enough. Other tribal businesses, the same. Convert them into ordinary corporations. Indian country? Allot the land among the tribal members, giving them an ordinary title (with no restrictions, the same as anyone else). For lands not suitable for individual allotment (such as forested mountain terrain), once again, form ordinary corporations with the tribal members as shareholders. As for the tax exemptions, those all need to go. Special hunting and fishing rights, the same. The criminal laws should protect and apply to the Indians like anyone else.

The Indians wouldn't exit such a deal without substantial resources, but the same can't be said for the tribes. Indian tribal sovereignty is no more than another word for Indian special privileges. To do away with the one, you have to do away with the other. So as governments, the tribes need to go out of existence. If they so desire, let them linger around as some sort of civic or cultural institutions (or even businesses). But the only governments in America should be the federal and state governments. The only laws should be the federal and state laws.

What should be the end Indian law? It should end.

END